*Being a gathering of the waters of several states of mid-Atlantic—*
*Pennsylvania, Maryland, Virginia, West Virginia—waters of Poto-*
*mac's North and South Branches, of Shenandoah, and others of*
*influence—flowing from the heights of Allegheny, cleaving through*
*the Blue Ridge, absorbing from* Pain de Sucre *and the Catoctins*
*across the foot of the mountains—broadening, finally, and commin-*
*gling below Federal City with waters of Chesapeake Bay and the*
*ocean beyond . . .*

*And being, further, a flowage and commingling of peoples in this great*
*basin, from the red man, Susquehannock, Piscataway, Nanticoke,*
*from the wellsprings of Potomac habitation—to the first white eyes to*
*view, the first white feet to walk upon this green valley—Jesuit, John*
*Smith, Lord Calvert—the trickle growing to a flood tide of whites and*
*the blacks they brought with them—exploring, settling, inhabiting,*
*tilling, fighting, building, polluting, revolting, rebelling, governing,*
*designing, cultivating, conserving, rioting . . . these peoples flowing*
*as the Potomac's waters flow from sources to the sea—flowing from*
*the wellsprings of history, cleaving through the tangible past, into the*
*present . . .*

*the whole being writ and limned with scholarly grace and wisdom by*
*the many who took pains to record—with pen, graver, brush,*
*machines for typing and the making of photographs—their several*
*journies.*

# WATERS OF POTOWMACK
## *by* PAUL METCALF

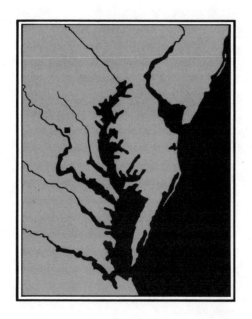

NORTH POINT PRESS · SAN FRANCISCO · 1982

Parts of WATERS OF POTOWMACK have appeared previously as chapbooks: THE ASSASSINATION, from Station Hill Press; and UPRIVER FARMING AND INDUSTRY, from Tansy Press. Other excerpts have appeared in the following periodicals: *A Hundred Posters, Attaboy!, Bezoar, Little Caesar, Periodics, Sarcophagus, Second Berkshire Anthology, St.Andrews Review, United Artists, Uzzano,* and *Winter.*

The publisher and author would like to thank The Library of Congress and The National Archives for their assistance with this project.

# Contents

Potomac's Valley shall become
a domain we create, an inchoate
scene where snows wane
and bulbs burn under the winter ground.
                                    Jonathan Williams

# Imprimis

*they are coming by water, drawing near in crafts and canoes    the river full of swarms of small fry, where fishes spawn in shoals    bushy or brushy river    traveling traders    river of swans    the burning pine, resembling a council fire*

Such are the suggested meanings of the Indian word *Potomac* (and the name itself, *Potomac,* may be found in twenty or more different spellings).

Above Great Falls, the river was known as *Cohongarootan* or Goose River, from the multitude of geese which frequented it in winter. *Shenandoah,* tributary to *Potomac,* may be Silver Water, River of High Mountains, River Through the Spruces, or still others, while Potomac's South Branch was called by Blue Ridge Indians *Wappa-tomika,* or River of Wild Geese.

———————

Three major streams—the North and South Branches and the Shen-andoah—converge to form the single river and tidal estuary now known as the Potomac. Bounded on the north by the watershed of the Susquehanna, on the west by that of the Ohio, on the south by the James and Rappahanock, and on the east by Chesapeake Bay, into which it flows, the Potomac River and basin cover an area of over one hundred thousand square miles—4 percent of the continental United States. Parts of Pennsylvania, Maryland, Virginia, and West Virginia, and the entire District of Columbia, are included in this area.

———————

Near Forty Three, between Brown and Backbone Mountains, not far from Blackwater Falls (where river waters run dark through coal beds and laurel thickets), a spring bubbles to the surface, flows northeastward, to Kempton, Difficult Creek, and Glade Run: the headfountains of Potomac. Wolfden Run and Elklick Run flow in; the waters pass Pee Wee and Horserock Hills, flow between Dans and Big Savage mountains, turn eastward and then southeastward around Piney Mountain, to Cumberland, Knobly Mountain, and the furthest northwestward diggings of the C & O Canal. Beyond Warrior Mountain to Oldtown . . .

> Shawnee Old Town, where Thomas Cresap settled in 1741 on an Indian wartrack, treated the Indians well, fed them generously.

The river embraces the South Branch, Sawpit and Purslane Runs, and turns northeast again, to meander in the Paw Paw Bends. Past Doe Gully and Sideling Hill, to take in the wild Great Cacapon, and flow not far from Berkeley Springs . . .

> . . . where the Indians gathered, before the time of whites, at the warm springs, and observed the valley as a neutral area: Tuscarora, Shawnee, Delaware, Iroquois, Catawba, and Huron, some of them bitter enemies, coming from great distances, camping side by side on Cacapon and Sleepy Creek mountains, bathing together in the springs, without animosity.

The waters turn southeast again, passing near Broadfording on the Conococheague, and Falling Waters, circling around Terrapin Neck to flow not far from Bardane and Bolivar, then to burst from the mountains at Harper's Ferry and the embouchure of Shenandoah. Strongly southeastward, now, bubbling over Bullring Falls, past Catoctin Mountain, Stumptown and Point of Rocks, Sugarloaf Mountain and Ball's Bluff, to Blockhouse Point, the river enturbulates over Great Falls, and gentles again, beyond Stubblefield and Little Falls . . .

. . . where the Indians maintained fishing villages, on the terraced bluffs overlooking the river, or on the floodplain just above the current, the villages swept freely by every spring freshet.

. . . Cabin John, Horsepen Run, Snakeden Branch, and Difficult Run, in the broadening tidal estuary, flowing due south beyond the Federal City, then meandering in the wider reaches, absorbing creeks and runs *where the edge of the hill is    at the end of the hill    twisting in the lands    at the end of water    where one goes pleasantly    at the long tidal stream.*

Past Bull Run, Bull Town Cove, Blue Banks, and Bull Bluff, downstream with the *stream that scoops out banks,* to the tidal run where *it flows in the opposite direction.* Then *one goes on downward    the jutting of water inland    at the big tidal river.*

Winkedoodle Point is *pleasant or fair.* Piccowaxen Creek is *ragged, pierced or broken shoes.* At Manahowic Creek, *they are merry people,* and Chaptico Bay is a *big broad river.*

To Honest Point. Thicket Point. Tippity-Wichity Island. Yeocomico: *he, that is floating on water, tossed to and fro.*

> to Smith Point,
> Point Lookout . . .

> to the open Bay:

> Waters of Potowmack

# Part One

# Discovery and Indians

Amerigo Vespucci, 1497 . . . John Cabot, 1498 . . . Quexos, 1521 and 1525 . . . Verrazano, 1524 . . . Estevan Gómez, 1525 . . . John Rut, 1527. . .

These and others, sailing in the Atlantic north or south, may have seen and not reported—or failed to see, hidden in fog or darkness—the opening of Bahía de Madre de Dios: Chesapeake Bay.

But in 1570, brothers and novices of the Society of Jesus, together with an Indian, coasted northward from Santa Elena (South Carolina), and entered the bay.

Juan de la Carrera:

> Our Fathers and Brothers disembarked in a great and beautiful port, and men who have sailed a great deal and have seen it say it is the best and largest port in the world. So, if I remember rightly, the pilot remarked to me, It is called the Bay of the Mother of God, and in it there are many deep-water ports, each better than the next. I saw this port myself when I went with the Governor, as I will narrate later. It seemed to me (for as it looked to me and I was given to understand), it was about 3 leagues at the mouth, and in length and breadth it was close to 30. They say that at the end of it the other sea begins.

The Jesuit fathers and brothers sailed up the River James,

landed,

settled,

and were wiped out by Indians.

In 1588, Vicente Gonzales, Captain, bearing with him one Luis Gerónimo de Oré, sailed north from San Agustín (Florida), rounded capes Hatteras and Henry, entered the Bay of the Mother of God, and followed the westerly shore northward.

> As they continued to sail north, the land from the east jutted into the bay. . . . They discovered inlets and coves as well as rivers along the western shore. Then they came upon a large fresh-water river, which, where it entered the bay, was more than 6 fathoms deep. To the north there was very high land, with ravines, but without trees, delightful and free, which has the aspect of a green field and was pleasant to behold. On the south shore of this river the beach is very calm and is lined with small pebbles. Farther up on the south bank of the same river there appeared a delightful valley, wooded, and pleasant land which seemed to be fertile and adaptable to stock-raising and farming. The river was located in a latitude of 38°. They named it San Pedro.

Potomac's first white sighting . . .

--------

For many thousands of years before Captain Gonzales, fishing, hunting, wandering Indians roamed Potomac shores, one tribe succeeding another, until Piscataways, Nacostines, Nanticokes, and Potopacos settled on the Maryland side, and tribes of the Powhatan Confederacy on the Virginia shore. All were of Algonquin stock, and of a peaceful nature. They made permanent settlements or villages near the water, cultivated the soil, raised maize, beans, and tobacco, and ate massively of the oysters (a shell midden near Pope's

Creek, Maryland, covers 30 acres). They killed game with a throwing stick—*atlatl*—as well as with bow and arrow, and dined on bison, elk, bear, wolf, skunk, swan, eagle, hawk, and buzzard. Settlements, except for hunting camps, were confined to the shores of river and tributary, from the river mouth to the Great Falls. Inland there was forest, with an open growth of hardwoods, the browsing deer reducing underbrush.

Tidewater Indians were adept at the manufacture of stone implements. W. H. Holmes, archeologist, 1897:

> The primitive inhabitants of the crystalline highlands had to make use of massive forms of rock or of rude angular or slightly water-worn fragments, and the reduction of these to available sizes and forms was a difficult work. But the inhabitants of the lowlands were born to more fortunate conditions. The agents of nature—the floods—had with more than human intelligence and power selected the choice bits of rock, the tough quartzite, the flinty quartz, the tough and brittle lavas, the indurated slates, the polished jasper, and the beautiful flints, from all the cliffs and gorges of the mountains, and had reduced them to convenient sizes and shapes, and had laid them down in the beds of the shallow estuaries where through the subsequent rising of the land and the cutting of valleys they were found at the door of the tidewater lodge. . . .
>
> The greatest aboriginal bowlder quarry known, and the most important implements shops yet observed on the Atlantic slope, are located on Fourteenth street 2½ miles from the President's house. One of the most interesting native soapstone quarries in the great series extending along the eastern base of the highland from Massachusetts to Georgia is on Connecticut avenue extended, barely beyond the city limits; and the most important ancient village-site in the whole tidewater province is situated on Anacostia river within the city and little more than a mile from the capitol.
>
> The capital city is paved with the art remains of a race who occupied its site in the shadowy past.

Rhyolite from South Mountain, soapstone from Bull Run, quarries on Piny Branch of Rock Creek, at the mouth of Wicomico, on Potomac Creek on the island of Chopawomsic . . . Fracturing or flaking, battering or pecking, incising or abrading, to make celts, axes, pestles, arrowheads, drills, knives, hoes, picks, chisels, pipes, and foolish ornaments . . .

Many of the villages were stockaded for defense with posts of honey locust, the thorny branches intertwined. Although at peace with one another, the Powhatans lived in fear of the Monocans and Manahoacs from the upland; and the Piscataways were crowded by Susquehannocks and Senecas from the north.

According to George Alsop, 1666, the Susquehannocks were "a people cast into the mold of a most large and warlike deportment, the men being for the most part seven foot high in latitude, and in magnitude and bulk suitable to so high a pitch; their voice large and hollow, as ascending out of a Cave, their gate strait and majestick."

An Iroquoian tribe, the Susquehannocks were hunters, living on the fresh-water streams, descending in spring and summer to salt water for fish and oysters, and to prey on sedentary Piscataways. By the seventeenth century, they had reached Great Falls and were moving down both sides of Chesapeake Bay.

One of the Five Nations, the Senecas (no doubt reinforced by others of the Five), ranged and raided through eastern America, from their home in upper New York to the Mississippi and to Florida, attacking Susquehannock and Piscataway alike.

The lower Potomac Indians huddled on the tidewater shores, "a mere selvage woven upon the fabric of the wilderness."

––––––––––

Sherds, spalls, and shells by a spring of sweet water . . . mortars of quartzite, pestles of felsite . . . 618 skulls, found in an Accokeek ossuary . . .

To this day [1935], a very considerable number of people reside about Port Tobacco River, who are designated locally as "Wesorts," who claim Indian origin, and who evince, in many cases, Indian physical characteristics, and who are evidently of mixed ancestry, Indian, negro and white.

---

April 10, 1607, John Smith and company departed the West Indies, heading for Virginia. April 21, they were struck by a storm, and floundered four days, out of sight of land and with no bottom. At dawn April 26, they sighted land—Cape Henry—and sailed into Chesapeake Bay. Search was made for a site for permanent settlement. May 13, the ships, standing in six fathoms of water in the James River, were tied to trees on the shore, and the next morning men and supplies went ashore, to establish Jamestown.

The following year, Smith explored Chesapeake Bay.

The second of June 1608. Smith left the fort, to performe his discoverie: with this company.

| | | | |
|---|---|---|---|
| Ralp Morton. | | Anas Todkill. | |
| Thomas Momford. | | Robert Small. | |
| William Cantrill. | } Gent. | James Watkins. | } Sould. |
| Richard Fetherstone. | | John Powell. | |
| James Bourne. | | James Read, blacke smith. | |
| Michael Sicklemore. | | Richard Keale, fishmonger. | |
| | | Jonas Profit, fisher. | |

These being in an open barge of two tunnes burthen, leaving the *Phenix* at Cape Henry, we crossed the bay to the Eastern shore, and fell with the Iles called Smith Iles. The first people we saw were 2. grimme and stout Salvages upon Cape-Charles, with long poles like Javelings, headed with bone. They boldly demanded what we were, and what we would, but after many circumstances, they in time seemed very kinde. . . . Passing along the coast, searching every inlet and bay fit for harbours and habitations: seeing many Iles in the midst of the bay, we bore up for them, but ere wee could attaine, such an extreme gust of wind, raine, thunder, and lightning happened, that with great daunger, we escaped the raging of that ocean-like water. The next day . . . brought us to the river Wighcocomoco. The people at first with great furies seemed to assault us, yet at last with songs, daunces, and much mirth, became very tractable. . . . In crossing over from the maine to other Iles, the wind and waters so much increased with thunder lightning and raine, that our foremast blew overbord, and such mightie waves overwrought us in that smal barge, that with great labour wee kept her from sinking, by freeing out the water. 2 daies we were forced to inhabit these uninhabited Iles, which (for the extremities of gusts, thunder, raine, stormes, and il weather) we called Limbo. Repairing our fore sail with our shirts, we set saile for the maine. . . . But finding this easterne shore shallow broken Iles, and the maine for most part without fresh water, we passed by the straights of Limbo, for the weasterne shore. So broad is the bay here, that we could scarce perceive the great high Cliffes on the other side. 30 leagues we sailed more Northwards, not finding any inhabitants, yet the coast well watred, the mountains very barren, the vallies very fertil, but the woods extreame thicke, full of Woolves, Beares, Deare, and other wild beasts. . . . When we first set saile, some of our gallants doubted nothing, but that our Captaine would make too much hast home. But having lien not above 12 daies in this smal Barge, oft tired at their oares, their bread spoiled with wet, so much that it was rotten (yet so good were their stomacks that they could digest it), did with continuall complaint so importune him now to returne, as caused him bespeake them in this manner.

Gentlemen . . . what shame would it be for you (that have beene so suspitious of my tendernesse) to force me returne with a months provision, scarce able to say where we have bin nor yet heard of that wee were sent to seeke. You cannot say but I have shared with you of the worst is past; and for what is to come, of lodging, diet, or whatsoever, I am contented you allot the worst part to my selfe. As for your feares, that I will lose my selfe in these unknowne large waters, or be swallowed up in some stormie gust, abandon those childesh feares, for worse than is past cannot happen, and there is as much daunger to returne, as to proceed forward. Regaine ther fore your old spirits; for returne I wil not, (if God assist me) till I have seen the Massawomekes, found Patawomeck, or the head of this great water you conceit to be endlesse.

3 or 4 daies we expected wind and weather, whose adverse extreamities added such discouragements to our discontents as 3 or 4 fel extreame sicke, whose pitiful complaints caused us to returne, leave the bay some 10 miles broad at 9 or 10 fadome.

The 16 of June, we fel with the river of Patawomeck. Feare being gon, and our men recovered, wee were all contente to take some paines to knowe the name of this 9 mile broad river. We could see no inhabitants for 30 myles saile. . . . The cause of this discovery was to search a glistering mettal, the Salvages told us they had from Patawomeck . . . also to search what furres, metals, rivers, Rockes, nations, woods, fishings, fruits, victuals, and other commodities the land afforded, and whether the bay were endlesse, or how farre it extended. The mine we found 9 or 10 myles up in the country from the river, but it proved of no value. Some Otters, Beavers, Martins, Luswarts, and sables we found and, in diverse places, that abundance of fish lying so thicke with their heads above the water, as for want of nets (our barge driving amongst them) we attempted to catch them with a frying pan.

Lord De-La-Ware, 1611:

This is a goodly River called Patomack, upon the borders whereof there are growne the goodliest Trees for Masts, that may be found elsewhere in the World: Hempe better then English, growing wilde in aboundance: Mines of Antimonie and Leade.

1621, George Calvert, the first Lord Baltimore, established a colony in Newfoundland, called Avalon. 1623, he secured a charter, but on visiting the settlement in 1627 he found the climate unsuitable, and sailed for Virginia.

June 20, 1632, a charter was issued to his son, Cecilius Calvert, the second Lord Baltimore:

> Unto the true meridian of the first fountain of the river Pattow-mack, thence verging towards the south, unto the farther bank of the said river, and following the same on the west and south, unto a certain place called Cinquack, situate near the mouth of the said river, where it disembogues into the aforesaid bay of Chesapeake. . . .
>
> Also, We do GRANT, and likewise CONFIRM, unto the said Baron of BALTIMORE, his heirs and assigns, all islands and islets within the limits aforesaid, all and singular the ports, harbors, bays, rivers and straits belonging to the region of islands aforesaid, and all the soil, plains, woods, mountains, marshes, lakes, rivers, bays and straits, situate, or being within the metes, bounds and limits aforesaid, with the fishings of every kind of fish, as well of whales, sturgeons, or other royal fish.

Father Andrew White:

> On the Twenty Second of the month of November, in the year 1633, being St. Cecilia's day, we set sail from Cowes in the Isle of Wight, with a gentle east wind blowing. . . .

The first Maryland colonists, in the *Ark,* of 300 tons, and the *Dove,* of 50 tons . . .

> On the 3 of March came unto Chesapeake Bay, at the mouth of Patomecke. This baye is the most delightful water I ever saw, between two sweet landes, with a channell 4 : 5 : 6 : 7 : and 8 fathoms deepe, some 10 leagues broad, at time of yeare full of fish, yet it doth yeeld to Patomeck, w^ch we have made S: Gregories. This is the sweetest and greatest river I have seene, so that the Thames is but a little finger to it. There are no marshes or swamps about it, but solid firme ground, with great variety of woode, not choaked up with undershrubs, but commonly

so farre distant from each other as a coach and fower horses may travele without molestation.

Having now arrived at the wished-for country, we allotted names according to circumstances. And indeed the Promontory, which is toward the south, we consecrated with the name of St. Gregory, naming the northern one St. Michael's in honor of all the angels. Never have I seen a larger or more beautiful river. . . .

For the rest, there are such numbers of swine and deer that they are rather an annoyance than an advantage. There are also vast herds of cows, and wild oxen, fit for beasts of burden and good to eat, besides five other kinds of animals unknown to us. . . .

The soyle, which is excellent so that we cannot sett downe a foot, but tread on Strawberries, raspires, fallen mulberrie vines, acchorns, walnutts, saxafras etc: and those in the wildest woods.

Birds diversely feathered there are infinite, as eagles, swans, hernes, geese, bitters, duckes, partridge read, blew, partie coloured, and the like. . . .

That night, fires blazed through the whole country, and since they had never seen such a large ship, messengers were sent in all directions, who reported that a *Canoe,* like an island had come with as many men as there were trees in the woods. We went on, however, to Heron's Islands, so called from the immense number of these birds.

⟨geography⟩


*The North and South Branches of the Potomac come together just below Oldtown, Maryland, and some 75 miles further downstream the Shenandoah enters at Harpers Ferry, where Virginia, West Virginia, and Maryland converge. Other major tributaries are the Cacapon, Monocacy, and Anacostia Rivers, and Conococheague Creek.*

*Although not a major system, like the Mississippi and other western rivers, the Potomac is second in size only to the Susquehanna among United States rivers of the North Atlantic slope.*

# Early Settlement

So that he, who out of curiosity desires to see the Landskip of the Creation drawn to the life, or to read Natures universal Herbal without book, may with the Opticks of a discreet discerning, view *Mary-Land* drest in her green and fragrant Mantle of the Spring. Neither do I think there is any place under the Heavenly altitude, or that has footing or room upon the circular Globe of this world, that can parallel this fertile and pleasant piece of ground in its multiplicity, or rather Natures extravagancy of a superabounding plenty. For so much doth this Country increase in a swelling Spring-tide of rich variety and diversities of all things, not only common provisions that supply the reaching stomach of man with a satisfactory plenty, but also extends with its liberality and free convenient benefits to each sensitive faculty, according to their several desiring Appetites.

For fiſh the Riuers are plentifully ſtored, with *Sturgion, Porpuffe, Baſe, Rockfiſh, Carpe, Shad, Herring, Ele, Catfiſh, Perch, Flat-fiſh, Troute, Sheepes-head, Drummers, Iarfiſh, Creuiſes, Crabbes, Oiſters* and diuerse other kindes. . . .

*Eagles, wilde Turkeis* much bigger than Engliſh, *Cranes, Herons* white and ruſſet, *Hawkes, wilde Pigeons* (in winter beyond number or imagination, my ſelfe haue ſeene three or four hourse together flockes in the aire, so thicke that even they haue ſhaddowed the skie from vs), *Turkie Buffards, Partridge, Snipes, Owles, Swans, Geeſe, Brants, Ducke* and Mallard, *Droeis, Shel Drakes, Cormorants, Teale, Widgeon, Curlewes, Puits,* beſides other small birds, as Blacke birde, hedge ſparrowes, Oxeies, woodpeckers, and in winter about Chriſtmas many flockes of *Parakertoths.*

For my part I rather impute their fecundity to the prouidence of God, who for euery mouth prouideth meate, and if this increafe were not, the Naturalls would affuredly ftarue: for the Deere (they kill as doe wee Beeves in *England*) all the yeer long, neither fparing yong nor olde, no not the Does readie to fawne, nor the yong fawnes, if but two daies ould), *Beauers, Otters, Foxes, Racounes*, almoft as big as a *Fox*, as good meat as a lamb, *hares, wild Cats, muske rats, Squirills* flying, and other of three or foure forts, *Appoffumes*, of the bigneffe and likeneffe of a Pigge, of a moneth ould, a beaft of as ftrange as incredible nature. . . .

There are woosels or blackbirds with red shoulders, thrushes, and diverse sorts of small birds, some red, some blew, scarce so bigge as a wrenne. . . .

The wood that is most common is Oke and Walnut. . . . There is also some Elme, some black walnut tree, and some Ash. . . . Of walnuts there is 2 or 3 kindes: there is a kinde of wood we called Cypres. . . . By the dwelling of the Savages are some great Mulbery trees. . . . In some parts, were found some Chesnuts whose wild fruit equalize the best in France, Spaine, Germany, or Italy, to their tasts that had tasted them all. Plumbs there are of 3 sorts. The red and white are like our hedge plumbs: but the other, which they call *Putchamins*, grow as high as a Palmeta. The fruit is like a medler; it is first greene, then yellow, and red when it is ripe: if it be not ripe it will drawe a mans mouth awrie with much torment; but when it is ripe, it is as delicious as an Apricock.

Near the Anacostia, the bison were "found to be very good and wholesome meate, and are very easie to be killed," and on the estuary, "myriads of canvass back ducks which literally blackened the surface of the water."

The Air and Temperature of the Seasons is much govern'd by Winds in *Virginia*, both as to heat and cold, driness and moisture. . . . the Nore and Nore-West are very nitrous and piercing, cold and clear, or else stormy. The South-East and South hazy and sultry hot: Their Winter is a fine clear Air, and dry, which renders it very pleasant: Their Frosts are short, but sometimes very sharp, that it will freeze the Rivers over three Miles broad; now, the Secretary of State assured me, it had frozen cleer over *Potomack* River, over against his House, where it is near nine Miles over: I have observed it freezes there the hardest, when from a moist South East, on a sudden the Wind passing by the Nore, a nitrous sharp Nore-West blows; not with high Gusts, but with a cutting brisk Air; and those Vales then that seem to be shelter'd from the Wind, and lie warm, where the Air is most stagnant and moist, are frozen the hardest, and seized the soonest; and there the Fruits are more subject to blast than where the Air has a free Motion. Snow falls sometimes in pretty Quantity, but rarely continues there above a Day or two; Their Spring is about a Month earlier than in *England;* In *April* they have frequent Rain, sometimes several short and suddain Gusts. May and June the Heat encreases, and it is much like our Summer, being mitigated with gentle Breezes that rise about nine of the clock, and decrease and incline as the sun rises and falls. *July* and *August* those Breezes cease, and the Air becomes stagnant that the Heat is violent and troublesome. In September the Weather usually breaks suddenly, and there falls generally very considerable Rains.

----

From the journal of Henry Fleet,

Here I was tempted to run up the river to the heads, there to trade with a strange and populous nation, called Mowhaks, man-eaters, but after good deliberation, I conceived many inconveniences that might fall out.

On Monday, the 25th of June, we set sail for the town of Tohoga, when we came to an anchor two leagues short of the Falls, being in the latitude of 41, on the 26th of June. This place without all question is the most pleasant and healthful place in all this

country, and most convenient for habitation, the air temperate
in summer and not violent in winter. It aboundeth with all
manner of fish. The Indians in one night commonly will catch
thirty sturgeons in a place where the river is not above twelve
fathom broad. And as for deer, buffaloes, bears, turkeys, the
woods do swarm with them, and the soil is exceedingly fertile,
but above this place the country is rocky and mountainous like
Cannida.

The 27th of June I manned my shallop, and went up with the
flood, the tide rising about four feet in height at this place. We
had not rowed above three miles, but we might hear the Falls to
roar about six miles distant, by which it appears that the river is
separated with rocks.

---

*A note for the Adventurers memory, of such things as hee may (if he
please) carry with him, either for his owne better accommoda-
tion (on Ship-board, or for some time after his arrivall in Maryland) or for trade, according to his abilitie.*

*Provision for Ship-board.*
Fine Wheate-flower, close and well packed, to make puddings,
etc. Clarret-wine burnt. Canary Sacke. Conserves, Marma-
lades, Suckets, and Spices. Sallet Oyle. Prunes to stew. Live
Poultry. Rice, Butter, Holland-cheese, or old Cheshire, gam-
mons of Bacon, Porke, dried Neates-tongues, Beefe packed
up in Vinegar, some Weather-sheepe, meats baked in earthen
potts, Leggs of Mutton minced, and stewed, and close packed
up in tried Sewet, or Butter, in earthen pots: Juyce of Limons,
etc.

*Provision for trade in Virginia or Maryland.*
If he be minded to furnish himself with Cattell in Virginia, his
best way is to carry a superfluitie of wollen, or linnen cloth,
callicoes, sayes, hatts, shooes, stockings, and all sorts of clothing; of Wine, Sugar, Prunes, Raisins, Currance, Honey, Spice,
and Grocery wares, with which hee may procure himselfe

cattell there, according to the stocke he dealeth withall. About 4. or 5. Pound laid out heere in commodities, will there buy a Cow; and betweene 20. and 30. shillings, a breeding Sow. The like Commodities will furnish him with there, or in Maryland, with Hogges, Poultry, and Corne. Hee may doe well to carry a superfluity of Knives, Combes, and Bracelets, to trade with the women Natives; and some Hatchets, Howes, and Axes, to trade with the men for Venison, Fish, Turkies, Corne, Fawnes to store a Parke, etc.

### Provisions for his House.

Iron, and Locks, and Hinges, and bolts; etc. Mustard-seede, Glasse and Leade for his windows, Mault for beere, a Hogshead of Beefe or Porke; Two or three Firkins of Butter, a hundred or two of old Cheeses; a gallon of honey, Soape and Candles, Iron wedges, Pookes for Rennet to make cheese: a good Mastiffe, etc.

### Provision for Husbandry.

Seede Wheate, Rie, Barley, and Oates (the best way to preserve it from heating at sea, is to carry it in the eare) Kernells of Peares and Apples (especially of Pepins, Pearemaines, and Dusons) for the making hereafter of Cider, and Perry; the stones and seedes of all those fruits and rootes, and herbes, which he desireth to have. Good store of claver grasse seede, to make good meadow.

### Provision for Fishing and Fowling.

Imprimis, necessaries for a boate of 3. or 4. Tunne; as Spikes, Nayles, Pitch, Tarre, Ocome, Canvis for a sayle, Ropes, Anchor, Iron for the Ruther: Fishing-lines for Cod and Macrills, etc. Cod-hookes, and Macrill-hookes, a Seane or Basse-net, Herring-netts, Leade, Fowling-pieces of sixe foote; Powder and Shott, and Flint Stones; a good Water-Spaniell, etc.

### A direction for choice of servants.

In the taking of servants, he may doe well to furnish himselfe with as many as he can, of usefull and necessary Arts: A Carpenter, of all others the most necessary; A Mill-wright, Ship-

wright, Boate-wright, Wheele-wright, Brick-maker, Brick-
layer, Potter: one that can cleave Lath and Pale, and make Pipe-
staves, etc. A Joyner, Cooper, Turner, Sawyer, Smith, Cutler,
Leather-dresser, Miller, Fisherman, and Gardiner. These will
be of most use; but any lusty young able man, that is willing to
labour and take paines, although he have no particular trade,
will be beneficial enough to his Master.

---

North America is naturally a very beautiful country, & as for
Virginia & Maryland, if you but glance across the plains you
will see them covered with lofty trees & lovely orchards of
apples, pears, cherries, apricots, figs & peaches. Where there is
no timber, there are fine pastures, or land planted with tobacco,
grain, vegetables, & all the necessaries of life. You will see the
four great rivers meandering along, & from their tranquil,
peaceful course be unable to discern from whence they rise. . . .

Nothwithstanding, we finde by them of best experience, an
industrious man not other waies imploied, may well tend foure
akers of Corne, and 1000. plants of Tobacco; and where they say
an aker will yeeld but three or foure barrels, we have ordinarily
foure or five, but of new ground six, seven, and eight, and a
barrell of Pease and Beanes, which we esteeme as good as two
of Corne, which is after thirty or forty bushels an aker, so that
one man may provide Corne for five; and apparell for two by
the profit of his Tobacco. They say also English Wheat will
yeeld but sixteene bushels an aker, and we have reaped thirty;
besides to manure the Land, no place hath more white and blew
Marble than here. . . .

[Tobacco is] generally made by all the Inhabitants of this Province, and between the months of *March* and *April* they sow the
seed (which is much smaller than Mustard-seed) in small beds
and patches digg'd up and made so by art, and about *May* the
plants commonly appear green in those beds: in *June* they are
transplanted from their beds, and set in little hillocks in distant
rowes, dug up for the same purpose: some twice or thrice they

are weeded, and succoured from their illegitimate Leaves that would be peeping out from the body of the Stalk. They top the several Plants as they find occasion in their predominating rankness: About the middle of *September* they cut the Tobacco down, and carry it into houses (made for that purpose) to bring it to its purity. . . .

Having for 19. yeare served *Virginia* the elder sister, I casting my eye on Mary-land the younger, grew in amoured on her beauty, resolving like Jacob when he had first served for Leah, to begin a fresh service for Rachell.

Two years and upward have I enjoyed her company with delight and profit. . . .

Hath she been deflowered by her own Inhabitants, stript, shorne and made deformed; yet such a naturall fertility and comeliness doth she retain that she cannot but be loved. . . .

It is (not an Island as is reported, but) part of that maine adjoyning to *Virginia*, only separated from *Virginia,* by a river of ten miles broad, called *Patomack* river, the commodities and manner of living as in *Virginia,* the soyle somewhat more temporate (as being more northerly) many stately and navigable rivers are contained in it, plentifully stored with whol some springs, a rich and pleasant soile, and so that its extraordinary goodnes hath made it rather desired than envied, which hath been fatall to her (as beauty is often times to those that are endued with it).

Settlers attacking new ground, with a hoe tillage scarcely less primitive than that of the Indians, releasing topsoil to swamp the inlets, silt the estuary. . . .

———————

Following John Smith's discovery of the river, patents for land were taken out, 1,000 or more acres at a time, as far up as the Great Falls, the "ffreshes of Petomack." Settlers came in, indentured servants, and, "about the last of August came in a dutch man of warre that sold us twenty Negars." (John Smith)

Houses, courthouses, and churches were built, and there were parsons, "such as wear black coats, babble in a pulpit and roar in a tavern."

Settlement, however, was slow, and many of the patents expired, "the lands lapsing for wante of Seating." There were Indians:

> Few or none had bin the Damages sustained by the English from the Indians, other than occasionally had happen'd sometimes upon private quarrells and provocations, untill in July, 1675, certain Doegs and Susquahanok Indians on Maryland side, stealing some Hoggs from the english at Potomake on the Virginia shore (as the River divides the same), were pursued by the English in a Boate, beaten or kill'd and the hoggs retaken from them; whereupon the Indians, repairing to their owne Towne, report it to their Superiors, and how that one Mathews (whose hoggs they had taken) had before abused and cheated them, in not paying them for such Indian trucke as he had formerly bought of them, and that they took his hogs for Satisfaction. Upon this (to be Reveng'd on Mathews) a warr Captain with some Indians came over to Potomake and killed two of Mathewes his servants, and came also a second time and Kill'd his sonne.

Depradations continued; the settlers employed rangers:

> *A Journiall of our Ranging, Given by me, David Strahane, Lieut. of the Rangers of Pottomack.*
> *June 9th, 1692:* We ranged on Ackoquane & so back of the Inhabitants & thence South. We returned & discovered nothing.
> *June, the 17th:* We ranged over Ackoquane & so we Ranged Round Puscattaway Neck & ther we lay that night.
> And on the 18th came to Pohike & ther we heard that Capt. Mason's Servt. man was missing. Then we sent to see if we could find him & wee followed his foot about halfe a mile, to a house that is deserted, & we took the track of a great many Indians & we followed it about 10 miles & our horses being weary & having no provisions, we was forced to returne.

*June the 26th:* We Ranged up to Jonathan Mathew's hs. along with Capt. Masone, & ther we mett with Capt. Housely & we sent over for the Emperour, but he would not come & we went over to the towne & they held a Mascomacko [council] & ordered 20 of their Indians to goe after the Indians that carried away Capt. Masone's man, & so we returned.

*July the 3rd:* We Ranged up Neapsico, and so back of the Inhabitants, &c.

*July 11th:* We Ranged up to Brent-towne & ther we lay &c.

*The 19th:* We ranged up Ackotink & discovered nothing &c.

So we Ranged once in the week till the 20th Septbr: then we marcht to Capt. Masone's & ther we mett with Capt. Housely & his men, so we drawed out 12 of our best horses: & so we ranged up Ackotink & ther we lay that night.

*Sept. the 22d:* We Ranged due North till we came to a great Run that made into the suggar land, & we marcht down it about 6 miles & ther we lay that night.

*Sept. the 23d:* We marcht to the suggar land and the 24th we Ranged about to see if we could find the trace of any Indians but we could not see any fresh sign. The 26th marcht to Capt. Masone's & there I dismissed my men till the next march.

The sugar land!

Taking their Range through a Piece of low Ground about Forty Miles above the inhabited Parts of Patowmeck River and resting themselves in the Woods . . . observed an inspissate Juice, like Molasses, distilling from the Tree. The Heat of the Sun had candied some of this juice, which gave the Men a Curiosity to taste it. They found it Sweet and by this Process of Nature learn'd to improve it into Sugar. But these Trees growing so far above the Christian Inhabitants, it hath not yet been tried whether for Quantity or Quality it may be worth while to cultivate this Discovery . . . yet it has been known among the Indians longer than any now living can remember.

Beyond Great Falls, sugar maples: the first taste of upland . . .

⟨spruce knob⟩

*Rising high in the Alleghenies, the North Fork of the South Branch drains Spruce Knob, in West Virginia, at an elevation of 4,860 feet.*

# Upriver Exploration

John Smith, speaking to an Indian, 1613: "When we asked him what was beyond the mountaines, he answered the Sunne: but of anything els he knew nothing."

Robert Beverley spoke of the Blue Ridge as an horizon of mystery, distant mountains known to the average planter only because they "shew themselves over the tops of the trees."

Durand of Dauphiné, 1686, "went fifty leagues into the country & from there could see high mountains, like the Alps, covered with eternal snows. . . . From thence the lovely rivers watering Virginia flow."

Smith again: "Beyond the mountaines from whence is the head of the river Patawomeke, the Savages report, inhabit their most mortall enimies, the Massawomekes upon a great salt water, which by all likelyhood is either some part of Commada, some great lake, or some inlet of some sea that falleth into the South sea."

John Clayton reported to the Royal Society, 1688:

> The Heads of the Branches of the Rivers interfere and lock one with another, which I think is best expressed after the Manner that an *Indian* explained himself once to me, when I enquired how nigh the Rivers of *Carolina, Virginia* and *Maryland* arose out of the Mountains, from those that ran Westerly on the other Side of the Mountains, he clapt the fingers of one Hand 'twixt those of the other, crying, they meet thus; the Branches of different Rivers rising not past a hundred Paces distant one from

another: So that no Country in the World can be more curiously
watered.

---

John Lederer, 1669:

The fourteenth of March, from the top of an eminent hill, I first
descried that Apalataean mountains, bearing due west to the
place I stood upon: their distance from me was so great, that I
could hardly discern whether they were mountains or clouds,
until my Indian fellow travelers prostrating themselves in ado-
ration, howled out after a barbarous manner, *Okée paeze* i.e.
God is nigh.

The eighteenth of March, after I had in vain assayed to ride up, I
alighted, and left my horse with one of the Indians, whilst with
the other two I climbed up the rocks, which were so incumbered
with bushes and brambles, that the ascent proved very difficult:
besides the first precipice was so steep, that if I lookt down I
was immediately taken with a swimming in my head. . . . The
height of the mountain was very extraordinary . . . but to the
north and west, my sight was suddenly bounded by mountains
higher than that I stood upon. . . .

The ascent was so steep, the cold so intense, and we so tired,
that having with much ado gained the top of one of the highest,
we drank the king's health in brandy, gave the mountain his
name, and agreed to turn back again, having no encouragement
from that prospect to proceed to a further discovery; since from
hence we saw another mountain, bearing north and by west to
us, of a prodigious height.

---

September 1716, the Huguenot John Fontaine accompanied Governor Alexander Spotswood and the Knights of the Golden Horseshoe
on an expedition to the Blue Ridge:

*3d.*—About eight we were on horseback, and about ten we
came to a thicket, so tightly laced together, that we had a great

deal of trouble to get through; our baggage was injured, our clothes torn all to rags, and the saddles and holsters also torn.

*4th.*—We crossed one of the small mountains this side the Appalachian, and from the top of it we had a fine view of the plains below. We were obliged to walk up the most of the way, there being abundance of loose stones on the side of the hill.

*5th.*—A fair day. At nine we were mounted; we were obliged to have axe-men to clear the way in some places. . . . In some places it was very steep, in others, it was so that we could ride up. About one of the clock we got to the top of the mountain; . . . We drank King George's health, and all the Royal Family's, at the very top of the Appalachian mountains. About a musket-shot from the spring there is another, which rises and runs down on the other side; it goes westward, and we thought we could go down that way, but we met with such prodigious precipices, that we were obliged to return to the top again. We found some trees which had been formerly marked, I suppose, by the Northern Indians, and following these trees, we found a good, safe descent. Several of the company were for returning; but the Governor persuaded them to continue on. About five, we were down on the other side, and continued our way for about seven miles further, until we came to a large river, by the side of which we encamped. . . . We saw, where we were over the mountains, the footing of elks and buffaloes, and their beds.

*6th.*—We crossed the river, which we called Euphrates. It is very deep; the main course of the water is north; it is four-score yards wide in the narrowest part. We drank some healths on the other side, and returned; after which I went a swimming in it. We could not find any fordable place, except the one by which we crossed, and it was deep in several places. I got some grasshoppers and fished; and another and I, we catched a dish of fish, some perch, and a fish they call chub. The others went a hunting, and killed deer and turkeys. The Governor had graving irons, but could not grave anything, the stones were so hard. I graved my name on a tree by the river side; and the Governor buried a bottle with a paper inclosed, on which he writ that he took possession of this place in the name and for King George the First of England. We had a good dinner, and after it we got the men together, and loaded all their arms, and we drank the King's health in Champagne, and fired a volley— the Princess's health in Burgundy, and fired a volley, and all the rest of the Royal Family in claret, and a volley. We drank the Governor's health and fired another volley. We had several sorts of liquors, viz., Virginia red wine and white wine, Irish usquebaugh, brandy, shrub, two sorts of rum, champagne, canary, cherry, punch, water, cider, &c.

. . . celebrating thus the Shenandoah.

Ascending the North Fork of South Branch to Mouth of Seneca, up Seneca Creek and across the Alleghenies to the head of Cheat, northward by way of Backbone: the Seneca or Shawnee Trail, a trail along the Blue Ridge, a trail in the Valley. The Conestoga Path: southward out of Pennsylvania, across Great and Little Pipe Creeks to Monocacy, westward over the mountains, across Antietam Creek, fording the Potomac below Shepherdstown: a trade route, Potomac to Susquehanna, via Conococheague Creek and The Carolina Road: fording the Potomac at the mouth of Monocacy, passing east of the Catoctins and Bull Run Mountain to the branches of Occoquan, and continuing southwest.

There were Shawnees, "the Strange Indians that are at the head of Potomocke neare the mountaines," at Shawnee Old Town, where Thomas Cresap settled. Toward the south, the Valley was a Shawnee hunting ground. Old Town was on "the Track of Indian Warriors, when going to War, either to the Noward, or Soward." Delawares from the north and Catawbas from the south traveled this track, and there was a great battle at the mouth of Antietam Creek, another at Slim Bottom on the South Branch, and another at Hanging Rocks. In still another, at Painted Rock, near Harper's Ferry, the Catawbas buried a Delaware chief alive; later, they said that Swearingen's spring flowed from the pulsing of his heart.

At the Smoke Hole on the South Branch, Indians fished and hunted, burned fires to dry their meat on the ledges and in the shallow shelter caves in the cliffs. The smoke, protected by the high walls, hung motionless over the gorge, in a flat canopy.

The Iroquois chief Tachanoontia said, 1742: "We have the Right of Conquest, a Right too dearly purchased and which cost us too much Blood to give up without any reason at all. . . . All the World knows we conquered the several Nations living on the Susquehanna, Cohongoronto and on the back of the great Mountains in Virginia. They feel the effects of our conquests, being now a part of our Nation and their lands at our disposal." Champlain's map of New France (1632) shows the correct topography of the Shenandoah Valley: no doubt the work of Jesuits accompanying the Iroquois on hunting parties.

There were burial mounds in the Shenandoah Valley: near Luray, skeletons of an Indian and a buffalo, side by side; in the alluvial bottom of Pass Run, a human skull and eight shark's teeth; on the South Branch of Potomac near Brandywine, seven skeletons arranged like the spokes of a wheel; and near Martinsburg, the skeletons of giants, seven feet long, with three-foot thighs.

<hr />

REPORT OF THE COMMISSIONERS TO
LAY OUT THE BOUNDS OF THE NORTHERN NECK

To the Hon^ble William Gooch Esq, his Majestys Lieutenant Governor and Commander in Chief of the Colony and Dominion of Virginia

The Underwritten Commissioners appointed by your Honour in Obedience to the Orders of his Majesty in his Privy Council of the 29th of November 1733 for Surveying and settling the Boundaries of that Tract of Territory of Land granted by the Crown to the Ancestors of the Right Honourable Thomas Lord Fairfax and under whom his Lordship now claims, Do humbly beg Leave to lay before your Honour the following Report of their Proceedings. . . .

. . . . . . . . . . . . . . . . . . . . . . . . . . . . . . . . . . . . . . . . . . . . . . . . . . . . . . . . . . . . .

We desired to know of my Lords Commissioners what they demanded in his Lordships Name as the Bounds of his grant?

To which they answer'd, that he claimed all the land contain'd within the South Branch of Rappahannock River, and the main branch of Potowmack as high as the head Springs thereof.

. . . . . . . . . . . . . . . . . . . . . . . . . . . . . . . . . . . . . . . . . . . . . . . . . . . . . . . . . .

Then in Conjunction with my Lords Commissioners We directed the main Branch of Powtomack River called Cohaungorooton to be Survey'd to the head Spring thereof, and appointed Mr Mayo and Mr Brookes whom we thought Equal to the difficult Service on the part of His Majesty; To these were join'd Mr Winslow and Mr Savage for the Lord Fairfax. These being all first sworn, were order'd by their Several Warrants to begin at the Confluence of that River with Sharando, and from thence to run the Courses, and Measure the Distances thereof to its first Spring; and of all this to return an Exact Plat, shewing all the Streams runing into the same on either side, together with a fair Copy of their Field-Notes. We also directed them to take the Latitude, and observe particularly where the said River intersects the 40th Degree

And to enable them to perform this arduous Work, We allotted them a Sufficient Number of Men for their Assistance and Defence, and a Competent Quantity of Provisions for their Subsistence

. . . . . . . . . . . . . . . . . . . . . . . . . . . . . . . . . . . . . . . . . . . . . . . . . . . . . . . . . .

The Lands at and near the Falls, were not granted till about the year 1709, nor can we find by any Evidence, that it was so much as known that the River ran thro' the great Ridge of Mountains till several Years after that

By the Map, you may please to observe that the River Potowmack divides itself into two Branches, just beyond the blue Mountains, there the main River loses its name, and the North Branch, which is much the larger, is call'd by the Indians Cohungorooton, and the other Sharando, as therefore the name of Potowmack ceases at this Confluence, and the Branches into which its Waters are divided have quite other Names, The Fork may not improperly be called the head thereof.

In the Year 1730 a Good Number of foreign Protestants were encouraged by the Government to settle beyond the Mountains, in order to strengthen our Frontiers on that Side; And they discover'd some distance up each of the aforemention'd branches, But none of thes discoverys very far, till the Surveyor sent out by us the last Fall, trac'd the River Cohungorootun quite up to the

Head Spring, which he found according to the Meanders thereof
to be above two hundred Miles from its confluence with Sharando.

. . . . . . . . . . . . . . . . . . . . . . . . . . . . . . . . . . . . . . . . . . . . . . . . . . . . . . . . . .

   But if his Lordship be allow'd to extend his Boundary from
the head of Conway River to the Head Spring of Cohungorootun, including the great and little Fork of Rappahannock, he will
then have at least five Millions two hundred eighty two thousand
Acres within his Grant. . . .

All which is most humbly submitted by

Sir      Your Honours most humble Servants

W. BYRD

JOHN ROBINSON

JOHN GRYMES

*Williamsburgh,* August 10th 1737

From a letter by William Byrd,

And here I think I ought to do Justice not only to the uncommon
Skill, but also to the Courage and Indefatiguable Industy of
Majr. Mayo and two of the other Surveyors, employ'd in this
long and difficult Task. Neither the unexpected Distance, nor
the Danger of being doubly Starved by Hunger and excessive
Cold, could in the least discourage them from going thro' with
Their Work, tho' at one time they were almost reduced to the
hard necessity of cutting up the most useless Person among
them, Mr. Savage, in order to Support and save the lives of the
rest. But Providence prevented that dreadful blow by an unexpected Supply another way, and so the Blind Surveyor escapt.

The field notes of this survey, to the headwaters of the Potomac, are
lost. A second survey was made in 1746 by one Thomas Lewis, who
made notes with a quill pen, in a tiny notebook, 3½ by 5⅝ inches:

JOURNAL 1746

From head Rappahannock to
head of Potomak running

Fairfax Boundary
. . . . . . . . . . . . . . . . . .

Wenesday September 10th 1746

Set out from home in order to wait on
his majestys & the Right Hounrable Thomas
Lord Fairfax Comisioner at Capt Downs
from Thence to proceed to Run the Dividing
Line Between his majesty and Ld Fairfax
from the head Spring of Rappahonock to
the head Spring of the North Branch
of Potowmack. Lay at Michael Wood
this night having Rod about 20 miles

Tuesday 16th    Spent the Day
in preparing for our Journey &c
in the Evening Retired to our Camp
where we spent our hours with
a great Deal of pleasure & meriment
was taken I'll in the night violent
Vomiting &c

Wensday 17th. . . . . .
. . . . . . . . . . . . . . This night
we were alarmed with a Quarrall
that happened in Capt Downs lane
amongst a Crowd of Drunken peple
the Rails & Staks of Capt Downs
fence Supply'd the want of Cudgels
which they apply'd with tolerable
good Sucses

Saturday 20th    the mountains made
Such a Dismal appearance that John
Thomas one of our men took Sick on
the Same & So Returned home.

. . . . . . . . . . . . . . . Returned to
our Camp very much Fautaug'd
Several horss very much hurt amongst
the Rocks on the mountain.

N 22½ (18) pole the Fork of the midle

Branch 34 poles &
N 10 W. 126 poles
. . . . . . . . . . . . . . . . . . .
N 10 E 60 po to the higest water near
the top of the mountain

1000 X a Br. Call'd the fountain of life
from the Seasonable Relive it was to us
the Day Being Exceding hot ye mountain
very high & Steep we were allmost over
-come & Ready to faint for want of
Water

Friday 3d Began at ye End of 1640
pole Run the Day Before Thence
604 pole ye top of y Divels Back Bone
alias the north mountain a Chestnut oak
md 31 miles.
824 X a Br. of Shand Runs to left
1104 pole left off & Encampd on ye
Comisioners & Baggage Could Come up
this Day Several of the horses had like Been
killd. tumbling over Rocks and precipices
& ourselves often in the outmost Danger
this tirable place was Call'd Purgatory
. . . . . we at length got to the Bottom nor
was our Case then much Better there Being
a large Water Course the Banks Extremly
Steep wc the neightborhood of the mountn
obliged us to Cross very often at places or
Banks allmost perpendicular. afer
a great Whiles Dispair we at length got
about 10 oClock
to our camp. hardly any of us Escaping
without Broken Shins or Some other miss
-fortune.

Being
along the mountains      prodigiously full of
fallen Timber & Ivey as thick as it Could
grow So Interwoven that horse or man Could

hardly force his way through it. So that we
had very Difficult access to the top of the Alleg-
haney mountain where was a precipice about
16 feet high & were very hard Set to get a place
where there was any probeability of our ascending
when we had gain'd the Sumit there was a
Level as fur as we Could see to Right & left
Clear of timber about a Quarter of a mile wide
Covered with Large flat Rocks & marshey
tho on the tope of the highest mountain I ever
Saw

. . . Roots together with the pines are Spread
over the Rocks & under the moss like arches In
what Danger must we be, in such a place all
Dangerous places being Obscured under a
Clock of moss Such thickets of Loral to Strugle
with whose Branches are all most as Obstinate
as if Composed of Iron.

     Thursday 16       Lay By in order to Rest
and Refresh our Selves & horses who were very
much Fatigued & Cripled one of our men
kill'd a Deer.

884 poles through the Swamp
1014 pole another Swamp Begins
1054 poles aLarge Creek Runs to the
Right which we Concluded to be the
Waters of Potowmack
1094 Total for the Day & fare Side the
     Swamp. here we Encamp'd

     The land or Soil on the N. W. Side the
River is Black & very moist a great
many Small Springs and Ouzey places
& prety Stoney & hilley Exceding well
timbred with Such as very Large
Spruce pines great multituds of Beach
and Shugartrees Chery trees the most
and finest I ever Saw Some three or
four foot Diameter thirty or forty
foot without a Branch. Some few

oaks Chestnuts and Locusts tho'
not maney &c

East 26 poles
S 71 E 31 poles
S 83 E 27 poles
S 80 E 6 poles to the Spring head
where we found the Following old
marks to (viz.) a Spruce pine
md RB. BW. IF. BL. FF. 1736
A Beach P.G. 1736 A Beach JS. &a
Black a Beach W.MAYO. two
Beaches & two Spruce pines markd
with three notches three way Each
& one Large Spruce pine Blazed
three Ways
We Dined on a Loyn Roasted Vension
about three O'Clock at the Spring head
Drank his Majestys health.

> Philip Kennedy, 1853: "[We] rode on down the
> middle of the wild meadow, through green grass,
> knee-high, and waving gently in the summer
> wind, until we reached a small stream, whose
> banks were overgrown with osiers and other deli-
> cate shrubs. This was the infant Potomac."

> Never was any poor Creaturs in
> Such ᵃ Condition ᵃˢ we were in nor Ever
> was a Criminal more glad By having
> made his Escape out of prison as
> we were to Get Rid of those Accursed
> Lorals.

---

George Washington, 1748 (age 16):

Saturday March 12    This morning Mr. James Genn ye. surv-
eyer came to us we travell'd ofer ye Blue Ridge to Capt. Ashby
on Shannondoah River, Nothing remarkable happen'd

Sunday March 13 . . . We went through most beautiful Groves of Sugar Trees and spent ye. best part of y. Day in admiring ye. Trees and richnes of ye Land

Monday 14th . . . (The Land exceeding Rich and Fertile all ye. way produces abundance of Grain Hemp Tobacco &ca.). . . .

Fryday 18th We Travell'd up about 35 Miles to Thomas Barwicks on Potomack where we found y. River so excessively high by Reason of y. Great Rains that had fallen up about y. Allegany Mountains as they told us which was then bringing down y. melted Snow and that it would not be fordable for severall Days it was then above Six foot Higher than usual and was rising we agreed to stay till Monday we this day call'd to see y. Fam'd Warm Springs we camped out in y. field. . . .

Sunday 20th Finding y. River not much abated we in y. Evening Swam our horses over and carried them to Charles Polks in Maryland for Pasturage till y. next Morning

Monday 21st We went over in a Canoe and travell'd up Maryland side all y. Day in a Continued Rain to Collo Cresaps right against y. Mouth of y. South Branch about 40 Miles from Polks I believe y. worst Road that ever was trod by Man or Beast

Wednesday 23d Rain'd till about two oClock and Clear'd when we were agreeably surprised at y. sight of thirty odd Indians coming from War with only one Scalp We had some Liquor with us of which we gave them Part it elevated there Spirits put them in y. Humour of Dauncing. . . .

Tuesday 29th This Morning went out and Survey'd five Hundred Acres of Land and went down to one Michael Stumps on y. So Fork of ye. Branch on our way Shot two Wild Turkies.

March 31st . . . Lot 4th this Lot survey'd myself Beginning at a Pine by a Rock. . . .

APRIL

Sunday 3d    Last Night was a much more blostering night than
ye. former we had our Tent Carried Quite of with ye. Wind.

---

*To the Right Honourable the Lords Commissioners of Trade and
Plantations*

*The humble Petition of Jacob Stauber, John Ochs, Ezekiel Harlan
and Thomas Gould*

Sheweth

That the said Jacob Stauber and Ezekiel Harlan having lived
upwards of twenty years in Pennsilvenia, following Husbandry
of which they have a perfect understanding, and also are well
acquainted with the nature of the land in those parts, and what it
is most capable of producing.

That the said Jacob Stauber hath lately taken a Journey into
Virginia on purpose to make a search after some uninhabited
Land behind the Mountains of that Province, which are about
thirty Miles over, and but one place fit to make a road, after he
had passed these Mountains with much pains, great difficulty
and hazard of Life without any Company or seeing any Indian in
all his Travells, he spent three Months time to View the Soyl and
Situation of the Land lying Westward to the said Mountains
towards Missisipy River, which Land he found to be good Pasture Ground fitt for planting of Vineyards on the side of the
Mountains and a very good Soyle for Hemp, Flax, and all sorts
of Grain, a proper climate to produce Silk. . . .

In Consideration of these Advantages, if Your Lordships
would be pleased to approve off y* same and influence that the
Government would be graciously pleased to grant a Joint Patent
for a Free Grant for the following Tract of Land to your Petition-
ers and their Heirs for ever, to begin at the double Top Mountain
by Hawks Bill Creek including the Mountains through which
the road is to be made, to go thence Northwards in a line to the
Borders of Pensilvania and behind the same, to make the whole
breadth 200 Miles, thence in a Straight West line to the River
Missisipy. . . .

Also the great Expences of making a Road 30 Miles long
through the Mountains . . . the same must be Cutt in a
Rock. . . .

March 30th 1731

August 21, 1751, Colonel Burwell, president of the Council and
Commander-in-Chief of Virginia, wrote to the Board of Trade:
"Notwithstanding the Grants of the Kings of England, France or
Spain, the Property of these uninhabited Parts of the World must be
founded upon prior Occupancy according to the Law of Nature; and
it is the seating and cultivating the soil and not the bare travelling
through a Territory that constitutes Right; and it will be politic and
highly for the Interest of the Crown to encourage the seating the
Lands Westward as soon as possible."

1699, Giles Vandercastel and Burr Harrison set out from Stafford, in
Tidewater, for Conoy Island and Point of Rocks:

The Distance from the inhabitance is about seventy miles, as we
conceave by our Journeys. The 16th of this Instance Aprill we
set out for the Inhabitance and ffound a good track ffor five miles
all the rest of the daye's Journey very Grubby and hilly, Except
some small patches; but very well for horse, tho nott good for
cartes, and butt one runn of any danger in a fresh and then very
bad. That night lay at the sugar land, which Judge to be fforty
miles.
    The 17th day we sett the River by a small Compaise, and
found itt lay up N. W. by N. and afterwards sett it ffoure times
and alwayes ffound itt neere the same corse. We generally kept
about one mile ffrom the River.
    About seven or eight miles above the sugar land we came to a
broad Branch of about fifty or sixty yards wide: a still or small
streeme; itt took oure horses up to the Belleys, very good going
in and out.
    About six miles ffarther came to another greate branch of
about sixty or seventy yeards wide with a strong streeme making ffal with large stones, that caused our horses sometimes to
be up to their Belleyes and sume times nott above their knees; so
we conceave it a ffresh than not ffordable.

Thence in a small Treck to a smaller Runn, about six miles, Indeferent very.

And soe held on till we came within six or seven miles of the forte or Island, and then very Grubby and greate stones standing Above the ground like heavy [hay] cocks; then hold for three or ffoure miles, and then shorte Ridgges with small Runns untill we came to the forte or Island.

In 1712, Christopher de Graffenried "visited those beautiful spots of the country, those enchanted islands in the Potomac River above the falls. And from there, on our return, we ascended a high mountain standing alone in the midst of a vast flat stretch of country, called because of its form Sugar Loaf which means in French Pain de sucre."

Meshach Browning, when a small child, emigrated to western Maryland:

We went on in good order until we reached Sideling Hill, where the road was very rough and rocky: by and by we arrived at a very sideling place, with a considerable precipice on our left— the wheels struck a rock on the other side, and away went wagon, horses, and all down the hill, rolling and smashing barrels of rum, hogsheads of sugar, sacks of salt, boxes of dry-goods, all tumbling through one another, smashing the bed of the wagon, and spilling the rum, molasses, sugar, and all.

My frightened mother called out, "Where is Meshach?"— knowing that I was riding in the wagon when it turned the dreadful somerset. All was bustle and alarm, until at length I was found under some straw and rubbish, stunned breathless, mangled, and black with suffocation. . . . The wagon was broken to pieces, the left hind-wheel smashed, and entirely useless. The man applied the spilling rum to us in handsful, until life began to return; and as mother saw hopes of my returning to her bosom again, she became quieted.

1747, one James Caudy—or Coddy—settled on the Cacapon River, near "Caudy's Castle":

A fragment of the mountain, separated from and independent of the neighboring mountains, forming, as it were, a half cone, and surrounded with a yawning chasm . . . the eastern side is a solid mass of granite, directly perpendicular. . . . From its western side it may be ascended by a man on foot to within about ninety or one hundred feet of its summit. From thence the rock suddenly shoots up something in the form of a comb, which is about ninety or one hundred feet in length eight or ten feet in thickness, and runs about north and south. On the eastern face of the rock, from where the comb is approached, a very narrow undulating path is formed, by pursuing which, active persons can ascend to its summit. . . . Along the path a few laurel shrubs have grown out of the fissures of the rock.

. . . During Indian raids early settlers, led by Caudy, would race up the rock and lie in wait near the top ready to push Indians over the edge of the precipice into the gorge below as they struggled up in single file.

---

The first Germans to reach the Potomac were at the mouth of Antietam Creek in 1726. Fording the river, they moved up the Shenandoah Valley, but a few—"an eddy of emigration"—followed an old Iroquois trail, east of the Catoctins, up the North Fork of Goose Creek and into the Blue Ridge.

Early settlers on the South Branch were Red Ike Pancake, Uriah Blue, and Colonel Thomas Cresap, who settled at Shawnee Old Town on the Maryland shores of the Potomac, 1741—acquired land, built roads, traded with the Indians. They called him "Big Spoon." Cresap traveled to London, age 70 . . . took a second wife, age 80 . . . and survived to the age of 105.

⟨estuary⟩

*The main river is nearly 400 miles long, and the tidal estuary on the lower reaches covers 117 miles, with 200,000 acres of water surface. Although heavily silted through the years, the estuary is navigable to Alexandria and Washington, with a 24-foot channel maintained by the U.S. Army Corps of Engineers.*

# Tidewater Colonial

From the journal of Philip Vickers Fithian, tutor to the children of Councillor Robert Carter at Nomini Hall, Westmoreland County, Virginia, 1773–74: "The broad beautiful Potowmack looks smooth & unbroken as tho' it was fettered in Ice."

George Washington's diary, January 1760:

Friday, 18th. . . . The Misting continuing till noon, when the Wind got Southerly, and being very warm occasioned a great thaw. I however found Potomk River quite covered with Ice. . . . Sunday, 20th. . . . The wind continued Southerly the whole day, the Ground very soft and rotten.
Tuesday, 22nd. . . . The weather clear and cold. the ground hard and froze and the River block'd up again.
Kill'd 17 more Hogs. . . .
Monday, 28th. The River clos again and the ground very knobby and hard.

Again, Washington:

1770 [JANUARY]
*Where & how my time is spent*
1. At home all day alone.
2. At home all day. Mr. Peake dined here.
3. At home all day alone.
4. Went a hunting with Jno. Custis and Lund Washington. Started a Deer and then a Fox, but got neither.
5. Rid to Muddy hole and Doeg Run. Carrd. the Dogs with me, but found nothing. Mr. Warnr. Washington and Mr. Thruston came in the Evening.

6. The two Colo. Fairfax's and Mrs. Fairfax dined here, as did Mr. Alexander and the two Gentn. that came the day before. The Belvoir Family returned after Dinner.

7. Mr. Washn. and Mr. Thruston went to Belvoir.

8. Went a huntg. with Mr. Alexander, J. P. Custis and Ld. W—n. Killd a fox (a dog one) after 3 hours chase. Mr. Alexr. went away and Wn. and Thruston came in ye aftern.

9. Went aducking, but got nothing, the Creeks and Rivers being froze. Mr. Robt. Adam dined here and returnd.

10. Mr. W–n. and Mr. Thruston set of home. I went a hunting in the Neck and visited the Plantn. there. Found and killd a bitch fox, after treeing it 3 times and chasg. it abt. 3 Hrs.

11. At home all day alone.

Fithian again:

Teusday 14.
The Weather vastly fine! There has been no rain of consequence nor any stormy or disagreeable Weather, since about the 10.ᵗʰ of last Month! From the Window, by which I write, I have a broad, a diversified, and an exceedingly beautiful Prospect of the high craggy Banks of the River *Nominy!* Some of those huge Hills are cover'd thick with *Cedar,* & Pine Shrubs; A vast quantity of which seems to be in almost every part of this Province— Others are naked, & when the Sun Shines look beautiful! At the Distance of about 5 Miles is the River Potowmack over which I can see the smoky Woods of Maryland. . . . Between my window and the potowmack, is Nominy Church, it stands close on the Bank of the River Nominy, in a pleasant agreeable place.

Sunday 3.
The country begins to put on her Flowery Garment, & appear in *gaity*—The *Apricots* are in their fullest Bloom; Peaches also, & Plumbs, & several sorts of Cheries are blossoming; as I look from my Window & see Groves of Peach Trees on the Banks of Nomini: (for the orchards here are very large) and other Fruit Trees in Blossom; and amongst them interspers'd the gloomy

Savin; beyond these at great Distance the blue Potowmack; and over this great River, just discern the Woods of Maryland.

From the journal of John Mercer, kept at his plantation at Marlborough, Stafford County, Virgina, 1767:

|  | *Temp.* |  |  |
|---|---|---|---|
| **March** |  |  |  |
| 21 | 64–63 | Daffodil |  |
|  |  | Hyacinths 6 |  |
|  |  | Violet |  |
|  |  | Narcissous |  |
| 22 | 60–69 | Almond |  |
|  |  | Apricot |  |
| 30 | 45–48 | May Cherry |  |
|  |  | Cucumber hotbed |  |
| 31 | 44–52 | Beans |  |
|  |  | Pease |  |
| **April** |  |  |  |
| 1 | 47–48 | Dwarf Iris |  |
| 2 | 41–52 | Cowslips |  |
| 3 | 44–50 |  | rain all night & morn |
| 7 | 44–50 | Wild curran |  |
| 9 | 48–32 | Asparagus |  |
|  |  | Radishes |  |
| 13 | 54–62 | Pear |  |
|  |  | Wall flower |  |
| 15 | 48–53 | Frittillary |  |
| 16 | 46–60 | Green Sagia |  |
| 17 | 48–55 | Prickson |  |
| 20 | 34–60 | Catchfly Julia |  |
| 30 | 64–70 | Parrot Tulip |  |
| **May** |  |  |  |
| 3 | 53–57 | Mourn[g] bride | rain in the night |
| 4 | 55–63 | Purple Stocks | D[o] in the night & Morn. |

| 8 | 59–72 | Horsechestnut Snow drop | |
| 15 | 60–76 | Corn Hay | fine rain in the night |
| 21 | 75–80 | Sm¹ bl. Iris | |
| June | | | |
| 5 | 70–64 | Jessamine | a fine rain |
| 17 | 75–82 | Yucca African Marigold | |
| July | | | |
| 5 | 70 | Coxcomb | rain all day |
| 16 | 73–76 | Marvel of Peru | |
| 23 | 76–85 | Sunflower | |

Fithian:

> I had the pleasure of walking to day at twelve o-Clock with M.ʳˢ Carter; She shewed me her stock of *Fowls & Mutton* for the winter; She observed, with great truth, that to live in the Country, and take no pleasure at all in Groves, Fields, or Meadows; nor in Cattle, Horses, & domestic Poultry, would be a manner of life too tedious to endure.

J. F. D. Smyth visited Tidewater Virginia, 1784:

> Several rich, moiſt, but not too wet ſpots of ground are choſen out, in the fall, each containing about a quarter of an acre, or more. . . .
>
> Theſe ſpots, which are generally in the woods, are cleared, and covered with bruſh or timber, for five or six feet thick and upwards, that is ſuffered to remain upon it until the time when the tobacco ſeed muſt be ſowed, which is within twelve days after Christmas.
>
> The evening is commonly choſen to ſet theſe places on fire, and when everything thereon is conſumed to aſhes the ground

is dug up, mixed with the afhes and broken very fine; the to-
bacco-feed, which is exceedingly fmall, being mixed with afhes
alfo, is then fown, and juft raked in lightly; the whole is immediately covered with brufh for fhelter to keep it warm. . . .

In this condition it remains until the frofts are all gone, when
the brufh is taken off, and the young plants are expofed to the
nutritive and genial warmth of the fun, which quickly invigo-
rates them in an astonifhing degree, and foon renders them
ftrong and large enough to be removed for planting, efpecially
if they be not fown too thick. . . .

The foil for tobacco muft be rich and ftrong. . . .

In the firft rains, which are here called feafons, after the
vernal equinox, the tobacco plants are carefully drawn while
the ground is foft, carried to the field where they are to be
planted. . . .

After the plants have taken root, and begun to grow, the
ground is carefully weeded, and worked either with hand hoes
or the plough. . . .

When it is ripe, a clammy moifture or perfpiration comes
forth upon the leaves . . . and they are then of a great weight and
fubftance.

When the tobacco is cut it is done when the fun is powerful. . . .

As the plants advance in curing the fticks are removed from
the fcaffolds out of doors into the tobacco house . . . being
placed higher as the tobacco approaches a perfect cure. . . .

The weight of each hogfhead muft be nine hundred and fifty
pounds neat, exclufive of the cafk.

Tobacco: grown on the plantations, cured, packed in hogsheads,
rolled down the rolling roads to the waterside, where every family
dock was an Atlantic port of call.

> Washington, to a London merchant: "I must once
> again beg the favor of you never to send me any Goods
> but in a Potomack Ship, and for this purpose let me
> recommend Captn. John Johnson. . . . Johnson is a

person I am acquanted with, know him to be very
careful and he comes past my door in his Ship."

Andrew Burnaby, 1759, remarked on "the cheapness
of land and the commodiousness of navigation: for
every person may with ease procure a small plantation, can ship his tobacco at his own door, and live
independent."

William Byrd: "Indeed people sail all these rivers with
merchantmen and arrive in front of the houses of the
merchants and planters in order to load and unload,
which serves commerce splendidly."

In Tidewater Potomac there are 98 navigable bays or
creeks: 49 on the Maryland shore, 49 on the Virginia
shore. . .

Burnaby:

The fruits introduced from Europe succeed extremely well;
particularly peaches, which have a very fine flavour, and grow
in such plenty as to serve to feed the hogs in the autumn of the
year. Their blossoms in the spring make a beautiful appearance
throughout the country.

Lord Adam Gordon, 1764-65:

They live on their Estates handsomely, and plentifully, raising
all they require, and depending for nothing on the Market. . . .
The houses are larger, better and more commodious than those
to the Southward. . . .
    They assist one another, and all Strangers with their Equi-
pages in so easy and kind a manner, as must deeply touch a
person of any feeling and convince them that in this Country,
Hospitality is everywhere practised. . . . Their provisions of
every kind is good, their Rivers supply them with a variety of
Fish, particularly Crabs and Oysters,—their pastures afford

them excellent Beef and Mutton, and their Woods are Stocked with Venison, Games and Hogs. . . . The Women make excellent Wives, and are in general great Breeders.—It is much the fashion to Marry young.

Tobias Lear:

The number of inhabitants living in the several counties of Virginia and Maryland, bordering upon the Potomack or its branches, amount to upwards of three hundred thousand, according to the census taken by order of the general government, in the year 1791.—They are all, or so nearly so, that not one fiftieth part can be excepted, cultivators of the soil. It is, therefore, easy to conceive, that they must send an immense quantity of produce to the shipping ports on the river. But, still so extensive is the country through which the Potomack and its branches pass, that it is yet but thinly settled.

Fithian:

Sup'd on *Crabs* & an elegant dish of Strawberries & cream— How natural, how agreeable, how majestic this place seems!
. . . we supt on Artichoks, & huckleberries & Milk—The toasts, after Supper, were the King; Queen & Royal Family, the Governor & his family, & then young Ladies of our acquaintance. . . .
Dined with us to day Captain Walker, Colonel Rich.^d Lee; and M.^r Lancelot Lee. Sat after dinner till Sunset, drank three Bottles of Medaira, two Bowls of Toddy!

Lord Gordon:

Poultry is as good as in South Carolina, and their Madeira Wine excellent, almost in every house; Punch and small Beer brewed from Molasses is also in use, but their Cyder far exceeds any Cyder I ever tasted at home—It is genuine and unadulterated, and will keep good to the age of twelve years and more.

(It became necessary for the Maryland assembly to pass legislation that indentured servants and slaves would be fed food other than oysters and terrapins several days each week.)

Durand:

> We decided to pass the night at Colonel Fichoux [Fitzhugh's], whose houses stand along the banks of the great Pethomak river. . . .
> He treated us royally, there was good wine & all kinds of beverages, so there was a great deal of carousing. He had sent for three fiddlers, a jester, a tight-rope dancer, an acrobat who tumbled around, & they gave us all the entertainment one could wish for. It was very cold, yet no one ever thinks of going near the fire, for they never put less than a cartload of wood in the fireplace & the whole room is kept warm. . . .
> The next day, after they had caroused until afternoon, we decided to cross this river. The Colonel had a quantity of wine & one of his punch-bowls brought to the shore.

And elsewhere, "It is a common law country. The laws are so wise that there are almost no law-suits. . . . When a man squanders his property he squanders his wifes also, & this is fair, for the women are foremost in drinking and smoking."

Fithian:

> There were several Minuets danced with great ease and propriety; after which the whole company joined in country-dances, and it was indeed beautiful to admiration. . . .
> M.ʳ *Carter,* & the young Ladies came Home last Night from the Ball, & brought with them M.ʳˢ *Lane,* they tell us there were upwards of Seventy at the Ball; forty-one Ladies; that the company was genteel.

Burnaby:

> Towards the close of an evening, when the company are pretty well tired with country dances, it is usual to dance jigs; a practice

originally borrowed, I am informed, from the negroes. These dances are without method or regularity: a gentleman and lady stand up, and dance about the room, one of them retiring, the other pursuing, then perhaps meeting, in an irregular fantastical manner.

Fithian:

The Dinner was as elegant as could be well expected when so great an Assembly were to be kept for so long a time.—For Drink, there was several sorts of Wine, good Lemon Punch, Toddy, Cyder, Porter &c.—About Seven the Ladies & Gentlemen begun to dance in the Ball-Room—first Minuets one Round; Second Giggs; third Reels; And last of All Country-Dances; tho' they struck several Marches occasionally—The Music was a French-Horn and two Violins—The Ladies were Dressed Gay, and splendid, & when dancing, their Skirts & Brocades rustled and trailed behind them!—But all did not join in the Dance for there were parties in Rooms made up, some at Cards; some drinking for Pleasure; some toasting the Sons of america; some singing "Liberty Songs" as they call'd them, in which six, eight, ten or more would put their Heads near together and roar. . . .

M.ʳ Carter informed me last Evening that this Family one year with another consumes 27000 Lb. of Pork; & twenty Beeves. 550 Bushels of Wheat, besides corn—4 Hogsheads of Rum, & 150 Gallons of Brandy.

Danced till half after two. . . . We got to Bed by three after a Day spent in constant Violent exercise, & drinking an unusual Quantity of Liquor; for my own part with Fatigue, Heat, Liquor, Noise, Want of sleep, and the exertion of my Animal spirits I was almost brought to believe several times that I felt a Fever fixing upon me, attended with every Symptom of the Fall Disorders—.

Advertisement in the *Virginia Gazette,* April 18, 1766:

The well known Horse
R A N T E R
WILL cover MARES this feason
at *Marlborough,* in *Stafford*
county, *Virginia,* at 40 s.
the leap, 4  1. for the feason,
and $1. to enfure a colt, *Virginia*
currency

Smyth:

There are races eftablifhed annually, almoft at every town and confiderable place in Virginia; and frequent matches on which large fums of money depend; the inhabitants, almoft to a man, being quite devoted to the diverfion of horfe-racing.

Very capital horfes are ftarted here, fuch as would make no defpicable figure at Newmarket: nor is their fpeed, bottom, or blood inferior to their appearance; the gentlemen of Virginia fparing no pains, trouble or expence in importing the beft ftock, and improving the excellence of the breed by proper and judicious crofling.

The gentlemen of fortune expend great fums on their ftuds . . . even the moft indigent perfon has his faddle-horfe, which he rides to every place, and on every occasion . . . indeed a man will frequently go five miles to catch a horfe, to ride only one mile upon afterwards.

Burnaby:

The horses are fleet and beautiful; and the gentlemen of Virginia, who are exceedingly fond of horse-racing, have spared no expence or trouble to improve the breed.

Lord Gordon:

Their Breed of Horses extremely good, and in particular those they run in their Carriages, which are mostly from thorough

bred Horses and country Mares,—they all drive Six horses . . .
going frequently Sixty Miles to dinner.

Fithian:

Loud disputes concerning the Excellence of each others Colts—
Concerning their Fathers, Mothers (for so they call the Dams),
Brothers, Sisters, Uncles, Aunts, Nephews, Nieces, & Cousins
to the fourth Degree!—All the Evening Toddy constantly
circulating—Supper came in, & at Supper I had a full, broad,
sattisfying View of Miss *Sally Panton*—I wanted to hear her
converse, but poor Girl anything she attempted to say was
drowned in the more polite & useful Jargon about Dogs &
Horses.

Beverley:

There is yet another kind of sport which the young people take
great delight in and that is the Hunting of wild Horses which
they pursue sometimes with Dogs and sometimes without.
You must know that they have many Horses foaled in the
Woods of the Uplands that never were in hand and are as shy as
any Savage Creature. These having no mark upon them belong
to him that first takes them.

In 1694, 1695, 1699, and 1712, acts were passed in the Maryland
assembly "to prevent the great evil of the multiplicity of horses in the
province."

———————

Fithian:

Rode to Ucomico Church—8 Miles—Heard Parson Smith.
He shewed to us the uncertainty of Riches, and their Insuffi-
ciency to make us happy. . . .
    The three grand divisions of time at the Church on Sundays,
Viz. before Service, giving & receiving letters of business,
reading Advertisements, consulting about the price of Tobacco,

Grain, &c. & settling either the lineage, Age or qualities of favourite Horses. 2. In the Church at Service, prayrs read over in haste, A Sermon seldom under & never over twenty minutes, but always made up of sound morality, or deep studied Metaphysicks. 3. After Service is over three quarters of an hour spent in strolling round the Church among the Crowd, in which time you will be invited by several different Gentlemen home with them to dinner. The Balls, the Fish-Feasts, the Dancing-School, the Christnings, the Cock fights, the Horse-Races, the Chariots, the Ladies Masked.

A Mr. Davis, teacher, circa 1800:

About eight miles from Occoquan Mills is a place of worship called Poheek Church. Thither I rode on Sunday and joined the congregation of Parson Weems, a Minister of the Episcopal persuasion, who was cheerful in his mien that he might win men to religion. A Virginian Churchyard on Sunday resembles rather a race-course than a sepulchral ground. The ladies come to it in carriages and the men make their horses fast to the trees. . . . I was confounded on first entering the Churchyard at Poheek to hear 'Steed threaten Steed with high and boastful neigh.' Nor was I less stunned with the rattling of carriage-wheels, the cracking of whips and vociferations of the gentlemen to the Negroes who accompanied them.

The building of Pohick Church:

ARTICLES OF AGREEMENT made this seventh day of April in the year 1769. Between the Vestry of Truro Parish in County of Fairfax, of the one part, and Daniel French of Fairfax Parish in the County aforesaid, Gent. of the other part, as follows, Vizt. The said Daniel French doth undertake and agree to build and finish in a workmanlike manner a Church, near the forks of the road above Robert Boggess's, to be placed as the Vestry shall hereafter direct . . . to be built of good bricks well burnt. . . . The corner of the House, the Pedistals, and Doors with the

Pediment heads to be of good white freestone, and the Returns and Arches of the Windows to be of rubbed brick. The Doors to be made of pine plank, two inches thick, moulded and raised pannells on both sides, and the frames thereof to be of pine clear of sap, with locust sills. The Window frames to be of pine clear of sap, with locust sills; the sashes to be made of pine plank one inch and three quarters thick; the Lights to be of the best Crown Glass, eighteen in each Window, eleven inches by nine; the Window and Door Cases to be made with double Archatraves. . . . The frame of the Roof to be of pine, except the King-Posts which are to be of oak; and the scantling to be of a size and proper proportion to the building. The Roof to be covered with inch pine plank well seasoned, and cyphered and lapt one inch and a half, and then with cypress shingles twenty inches long, and to show six inches. . . .

The Floors to be framed with good oak clear of sap, and laid with pine plank inch and a half thick, and well seasoned. . . . The Isles to be laid with flaggstone, well squared and jointed.

The Pews to be wainscoted with pine plank an inch and a half thick, well seasoned, to be quarter-round on both sides, and raised pannel on one side the seats to be of inch and a half pine plank, fourteen inches broad and well supported. The Altar Piece to be twenty feet high and fifteen feet wide, and done with wainscot after the Ionic Order. The floor of the Communion Place to be raised twenty inches higher than the floor of the House, with hand-rails and Bannisters of pine, and a Communion-Table of Black Walnut of a proper size. The Apostles Creed, the Lords-Prayer, and the ten Commandments to be neatly painted on the Alter-piece in black letters. . . .

The inside of the Church to be Ceiled, Plaistered and White-Washed; no Loam or Clay to be used in the Plaistering. The Outside Cornice, and all the Wooden-Work on the inside of the House (except the floors) to be neatly painted of the proper colours. Stone Steps to be put to the Doors, and locks and hinges; and hinges to the Pews, Pulpit and Communion Place.

The whole Building to be compleated and finished by the first day of September, which shall be in the year of our Lord, One thousand seven hundred and seventy two.

William Byrd:

Because navigation in Virginia is so easy and convenient, every year many hundred English ships come there from all points of the earth, in order to trade and bring, among other very useful things, many Negroes or black slaves to sell.

Fithian:

When I am on the Subject, I will relate further, what I heard M.ʳ George Lees Overseer, one Morgan, say the other day that he himself had often done to Negroes, and found it useful: He said that whipping of any kind does them no good, for they will laugh at your greatest Severity; But he told us he had invented two things, and by several experiments had proved their success.—For Sullenness, Obstinacy, or Idleness, says he, Take a Negro, strip him, tie him fast to a post; take then a sharp Curry-Comb, & curry him severely til he is well scraped; & call a Boy with some dry Hay, and make the Boy rub him down for several Minutes, then salt him, & unlose him. He will attend to his Business, (said the inhuman Infidel) afterwards!—But savage Cruelty does not exceed His next diabolical invention—To get a Secret from a Negro, says he, take the following method—Lay upon your Floor a large thick plank, having a peg about eighteen Inches long, of hard wood, & very Sharp, on the upper end, fixed fast in the plank—then strip the Negro, tie the Cord to a staple in the Ceiling, so as that his foot may just rest on the sharpened Peg, then turn him briskly round, and you would laugh (said our informer) at the Dexterity of the Negro, while he was relieving his Feet on the sharpened Peg!

George Washington:

Monday, 28th. . . . Found the new Negro Cupid ill of a pleurisy at Dogue Run Quarter and had him brot. home in a cart for better care of him.

Tuesday, 29th. . . . Darcus, daughter to Phillis, died, which makes 4 negroes lost this Winter; viz, 3 Dower Negroes namely—Beck,—appraised to £50, Doll's Child born since, and Darcus— . . . , and Belinda, a Wench of mine.

From Virginia laws and statutes:

I. FOR the better settling and preservation of estates within this dominion.

II. *Be it enacted, by the governor, council and burgesses of this present general assembly, and it is hereby enacted by the authority of the same,* That from and after the passing of this act, all negro, mulatto, and Indian slaves, in all courts of judicature, and other places, within this dominion, shall be held, taken, and adjudged, to be real estate (and not chattels;) and shall descend unto the heirs and widoes of persons departing this life, according to the manner and custom of land of inheritence, held in fee simple. . . .

XXXVII. And whereas, many times, slaves run away and lie out, hid and lurking in swamps, woods, and other obscure places, killing hogs, and committing other injuries to the inhabitants of this her majesty's colony and dominion, *Be it therefore enacted, by the authority aforesaid, and it is hereby enacted,* That in all such cases upon intelligence given of any slave lying out, as aforesaid, any two justices (Quorum unus) of the peace of the country wherein such slave is supposed to lurk or do mischief, shall be and are empowered to issue proclamation. . . . Which proclamation shall be published on a Sabbath day, at the door of every church and chapel, in the said county, by the parish clerk, or reader, of the church, immediately after divine worship: And in case any slave, against whom proclamation hath been thus issued, and once published at any church or chapel, as aforesaid, stay out, and do not immediately return home, it shall be lawful for any person or persons whatsoever, to kill and destroy such slaves.

Thomas Jefferson, writing in 1785:

There must doubtless be an unhappy influence on the manners of our people produced by the existence of slavery among us. The whole commerce between master and slave is a perpetual exercise of the most boisterous passions, the most unremitting despotism on the one part, and degrading submissions on the other. Our children see this and learn to imitate it; for man is an imitative animal. . . . The parent storms, the child looks on, catches the lineaments of wrath, puts on the same airs in the circle of smaller slaves, gives loose to the worst of passions, and thus nursed, educated, and daily exercised in tyranny, cannot but be stamped by it with odious peculiarities. The man must be a prodigy who can retain his manners and morals undepraved by such circumstances. And with what execration should the statesman be loaded, who, permitting one half the citizens thus to trample on the rights of the other, transforms those into despots, and these into enemies, destroys the morals of the one part, and the *amor patriae* of the other. For if a slave can have a country in this world, it must be any other in preference to that in which he is born to live and labor for another; in which he must lock up the faculties of his nature, contribute as far as depends on his individual endeavors to the evanishment of the human race, or entail his own miserable condition on the endless generations proceeding from him.

Burnaby:

From what has been said of this colony, it will not be difficult to form an idea of the character of its inhabitants. The climate and external appearance of the country conspire to make them indolent, easy, and good natured; extremely fond of society and much given to convivial pleasures. In consequence of this, they seldom show any spirit of enterprise, or expose themselves willingly to fatigue. Their authority over their slaves renders them vain and imperious.

Jefferson:

With the morals of the people, their industry is also destroyed.
For in a warm climate, no man will labor for himself who can
make another labor for him. This is so true, that of the proprietors of slaves a very small proportion indeed are ever seen to
labor.

Smyth:

In ſhort, take them all together, they form a ſtrange combination
of incongruous contradictory qualities, and principles directly
oppoſite; the beſt and the worſt, the moſt valuable and the moſt
worthleſs, elegant accomplishments and ſavage brutality, being
in many of them moſt unaccountably blended.

---

Byrd:

It is to be wondered at, that the Virginians devote themselves to
nothing else but tobacco trade, since they could plant many
more useful things.

Douglas Southall Freeman:

Mount Vernon has a sandy surface, and below that a heavy soil.
At a depth of eighteen inches to two feet, approximately, is the
clay pan. This accentuates both wetness and dryness. Precisely
the "right year" is required for good growing conditions. This
is not soil for wheat, and is still worse for tobacco.

Fithian:

And their method of farming is slovenly, without any regard to
continue their Land in heart, for future Crops—They plant
large Quantities of Land, without any Manure, & work it very
hard to make the best of the Crop, and when the Crop comes
off they take away the Fences to inclose another Piece of Land

for the next years tillage, and leave this a common to be destroyed by Winter & Beasts till they stand in need of it again to plough—The Land most commonly too is of a light sandy soil, & produces in very great quantities shrubby *Savins & Pines*.

Johann David Schoepf, traveling in Virginia, 1783-84:

> The Virginians of the lower country are very easy and negligent husbandmen. Much and very good land, which would yield an abundant support to an industrious family, remains unused when once a little exhausted, no thought being given so far to dunging and other improvements. New land is taken up, the best to be had, tobacco is grown on it 3–4 years, and then Indian corn, so long as any will come. And in the end, if the soil is thoroughly impoverished, they begin again with a new piece and go through the rotation. Meantime wood grows again on the old land, and on the new is at pains to be cleared off; and all this to avoid dunging and all the trouble involved in a more careful handling of their cattle, if dung is to be had.

Isaac Weld traveled in Maryland, 1796:

> From Port Tobacco to Hoe's Ferry on the Potowmac River, the country is flat and sandy and wears a most dreary aspect. Nothing is to be seen here for miles together but extensive plains that have been worn out by the culture of tobacco, overgrown with yellow sedge and interspersed with groves of pine and cedar trees, the dark green colour of which forms a curious contrast with the yellow of the sedge. In the midst of these plains are the remains of several good houses.

Abandoned tobacco lands—"old fields"—grown up in sedge, sassafras, and pine. There were also "poisoned fields"—land burned by the Indians, to improve the game.

On the Virginia side, the port of Dumfries grew, briefly flourished, and died; the inlet silted up, the land was abandoned.

---

Fithian:

The School consists of eight—Two of M.̲ Carter's Sons—One
Nephew—And five Daughters—The eldest Son is reading
Salust: Grammatical Exercises, and latin Grammar—The sec-
ond Son is reading english Grammar & Reading English: Writing and Cyphering in Subtraction—The Nephew is Reading
and Writing as above; and Ciphering in Reduction—The eldest
daughter is Reading the Spectator; Writing; & beginning to
Cypher. . . .
    Miss Nancy is beginning on the *Guitar*. Ben finished reading
Salusts Cataline Conspiracy.
    Spent most of the Day at the great House hearing the various
Instruments of Music.
    M.̲ *Stadley* played on the Harpsichord & harmonica. . . .
    M.̲ Carter has an overgrown library of Books of which he
allows me the free use. It consists of a general collection of law
books, all the Latin and Greek Classicks, vast number of books
on Divinity chiefly by writers who are of the established Religion; he has the works of almost all the late famous writers, as
Locke, Addison, Young, Pope, Swift, Dryden, &c.

And in the library of John Mercer at Marlborough, Stafford County:

Alian's Tactick's of War
Smith's Distilling & Fermentation
Greek Grammar
Greek Testament
Colgrave's French Dictionary
The Sum of Christian Religion
The Country Parson's Advice
History of the Turks 4ᵗʰ vol
Bradley's Hop Garden
Monarchy of the Bees
A Discourse of Sallets
Pocket Farrier
Acc.ᵗ of Society for Reformation of Manners
Atkinson's Epitome of Navigation
Salmon's Herbal 2 vol

Strother on Sickness & Health
Wiseman's Surgery 2 vol
Arbuthnot of Aliment
Andrey on Worms
Shakespears Plays 8 vol
Robert's Map of Commerce
The Musical Miscellany 6 vol
Mead on Poysons
Ovid's Art of Love

---

Fithian: "We had an elegant dinner; Beef & Green; roast-Pig; fine boil'd Rock-Fish, Pudding, Cheese &c—Drink: good Porter-Beer, Cyder, Rum, & Brandy Toddy. The Virginians are so kind."

# TURNING POINT: 1776

St. Mary's County, July 15th, 1776
Gentlemen:
This to inform you that there is now lying, off the mouth of
the St. Mary's River, between seventy and eighty sail of vessels.
I am now at Leonard Town on my way down with part of the
6th Battalion under my command, where I received an Express
from Col. Barnes (who is now at St. Inegoe's Neck with the
lower Battalion) informing me that this morning Ten Boats full
of men landed on St. George's Island and had returned for more.
I expect to be opposite the island some time this night and shall
endeavor to get the best intelligence I can of their numbers and
give the earliest notice. We shall want more powder and lead
and also flints, if they are to be had. . . .
Gentlemen: Your mo;obedt Servt

Jeremiah Jordan, colonel in the Maryland Militia, reported the appearance of the seventy-two vessels of the fleet under Lord Dunmore,
Royal Governor of Virginia. Writing again, July 17:

I think from all appearances the Fleet will continue some time,
if so, some Cannon and Swivels will be absolutely necessary to
dislodge the men they have landed on the Island. With what
assistance we can give in this quarter, I think 500 of the Militia
of the upper Battalions will be full enough to oppose the enemy.
We have now at different posts about 600 men. . . . Col. Barnes
with his Battalion is on the other side of the river, watching the
motions of the enemy there.

Major Thomas Price, reporting July 23 and 26:

> Three or four large ships went up the river the evening before I
> got here, since which a number of cannon have been fired as I
> suppose near the mouth of Nanjemoy. I have ordered the other
> two pieces of Cannon to the Lower Camp and shall as soon as
> the nine pounder arrives order that there and if intrenching tools
> which I have sent after can be had thro up an entrenchment. . . .
>      By the best advice I can get from the Prisoners and many
> deserters the whole fleet does not intend to stay here longer than
> those up Potowmack comes down which they expect every day.

Lord Dunmore's invasion was part of a larger plan. British Loyalists
were to incite the Indians to raise an army in Detroit, attack and seize
Pittsburg, and raid the back settlements of Virginia from there. A
stronghold was to be established at Cumberland, and Alexandria
was to be seized. Dunmore, with a fleet of ships and body of runaway
slaves, would meet them at Alexandria. The colonies would be split,
north and south, along the line of the Potomac.

Major Price wrote, "We have several Deserters from the Enemy
most of them in the small pox. . . . The shores are full of Dead
Bodies chiefly negroes. I think if they stay here any time they must
be ruined, for by Deaths Desertions and the Worm I think their
business must be done compleatly."

The western action did not materialize. Lord Dunmore raided as far
as Quantico, but he was harassed by local militia—and a violent summer storm on the Potomac. The British fleet never reached Alexandria.

For the remainder of the Revolution, the British raided waterfront
plantations:

> We have for some time past been ravaged in this County by the
> enemy. They on Friday last landed and plundered several fami-
> lies on Smith's Creek. . . .

Two of the enemy's vessels came up the Potomac on Thursday
last in the Evening. They dispatched two of their barges in the
night to plunder; the men from these landed at Port Tobacco
Warehouse. . . . From thence they crossed over to Mr. Walter
Hanson's and robbed him of all effects to considerable value.

On Friday morning they landed at Captain George Dent's
before the militia could be collected in sufficient force to oppose
them and burnt all his houses.

On the 13th a Brig with two Schooners appeared off the mouth
of St. Clement's Bay, and landed two barges loaded with men
at Mr. Herbert Blackestone's House, which they burned and
carried Blackestone with them, where he has continued.

The Americans offered suicide barges:

These barges were loaded with explosives and drifted down on
the anchored British fleet at night, which annoyed the British
no end. The men in the barges had little chance of escape because
the fuses could not be lit until the boats had made contact with
the fleet.

For many years after, the American Revolution was known in
southern Maryland as Lord Dunmore's War.

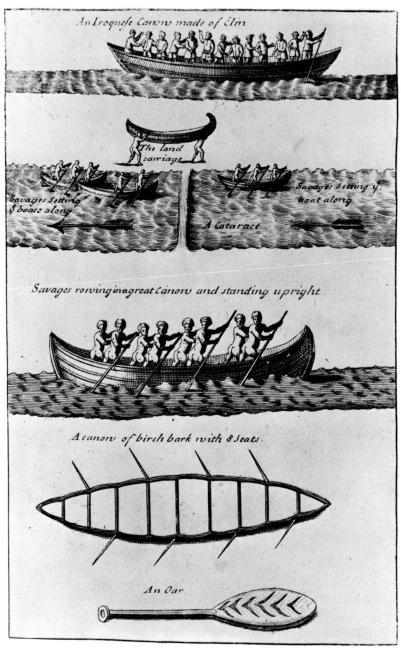

An early artist's rendering of Eastern Amerindian bark canoes.
*(The Library of Congress)*

*Above:* General Sheene's house on Fort Anne Creek, which was torched by General Burgoyne's army. *(The Library of Congress)* *Opposite:* The Indian village of Secotan on the Pamlico River, an engraving by Theodor DeBry. *(The Library of Congress)*

Plan for the city of Washington based on
L'Enfant's design. The plan shows clearly how
the city was constructed around the waters of
the region. 1792.

*Above:* The fenced city of Sasquesahanok.
*(The Library of Congress)*
*Opposite Top:* The earliest known photographic view
(daguerrotype) of the Capitol building, capped with
Bulfinch's dome. Ca. 1846. *(The Library of Congress)*
*Opposite Bottom:* Photographic view of the White House
attributed to John Plumbe, Jr. Ca. 1846.
*(The Library of Congress)*

Construction of the cast-iron dome of the
Capitol building. 1860. *(The National Archives)*

# Part Two

# Upriver Settlement

Andrew Burnaby, 1759, at the Great Falls:

The channel of the river is contracted by hills. . . . It is clogged moreover with innumerable rocks; so that the water for a mile or two flows with accelerated velocity. At length coming to a ledge of rocks, which runs diametrically across the river, it divides into two spouts, each about eight yards wide, and rushes down a precipice with incredible rapidity. . . . These two spouts, after running in separate channels for a short space, at length unite in one about thirty yards wide; and as we judged from the smoothness of the surface and our unsuccessful endeavors to fathom it, of prodigious depth. The rocks on each side are at least ninety or a hundred feet high; and yet, in great freshes, the water overflows the tops of them, as appeared by several large and entire trees, which had lodged there.

David Baillie Warden, 1816:

The wild and romantic scenery of the Great Falls, which are to be seen most to advantage from the Virginia side is scarcely to be equalled. There is a stupendous projecting rock covered with cedar, where one may sit and gaze at the waters dashing with impetuosity over the rugged surface. At the close of winter vast masses of ice, rolling over the rocks with hideous crash, present a scene truly sublime.

. . . Several delicious springs issue from a neighboring hill which commands an enchanting prospect . . . the yellow jessamine is of a prodigious size. The prickly pear grows on the banks. . . . White hore-hound and sweet-fennel, . . . the odour of aromatic plants, . . . wild cherries and strawberries.

George Washington, writing from Harper's Ferry, 1785:

> In my ride from George Town to this place, I made the following
> observations: The land about the first, is not only hilly, and a
> good deal mixed with flint stone, but is of an indifferent quality
> 'till we left the great Road (3 Miles from G:Town). . . . The
> quality of the land then improves, and seems well adapted to the
> culture of small grain, but continues broken and by no means in
> a high state of cultivation. . . . That about the Maryland Sugar
> Lands . . . which is five miles above Seneca, is remarkably fine,
> and very level. From thence to Monocasy about 12 miles further
> they are less level and of much inferior quality. That from
> Monocasy to Frederick Town (distant 12 or 13 Miles) nothing
> can well exceed them for fertility of Soil, convenient levelness,
> and luxuriant growth of Timber. The farms seem to be under
> good cultivation. . . .
> Frederick Town stands on a branch of Monocasy, and lyes
> rather low. The Country about it is beautiful and seems to be in
> high cultivation.

J. F. D. Smyth, 1784:

> The land around Frederick Town is heavy, ſtrong, and rich, well
> calculated for wheat, with which it abounds; this being as
> plentiful a country as any in the world.
> The face of the country here ſwells into beautiful hills and
> dales, and twelve miles beyond the town it ariſes into moun-
> tains, named the South Mountain. The ſoil is generally of a deep
> ruſty brown colour.

Burnaby, crossing the Blue Ridge:

> When I got to the top, I was inexpressibly delighted with the
> scene which opened before me. Immediately under the moun-
> tain, which was covered with chamoe-daphnes in full bloom,
> was a most beautiful river: beyond this an extensive plain, di-
> versified with every pleasing object that nature can exhibit; and,
> at the distance of fifty miles, another ridge of still more lofty

mountains, called the Great, or North Ridge, which inclosed and terminated the whole.

The river Shenandoah rises a great way to the southward from under this Great North Ridge. . . . it is exceedingly romantic and beautiful, forming a great variety of falls, and is so transparent, that you may see the smallest pebble at the depths of eight or ten feet.

Smyth, in the Shenandoah Valley:

This valley is about thirty miles wide, extending many hundred miles in length, and contains a body of the richest land in the world. It abounds with the moſt clear and pellucid water-courſes.

Washington, in the Paw Paw Bends:

This tract, though small, is extremely valuable. It lyes on Potomac River about 12 miles above the Town of Bath (or Warm Springs) and is in the shape of a horse Shoe: the river running almost around it. Two hundred Acres of it is rich low grounds; with a great abundance of the largest and finest Walnut trees. . . . [On the South Branch] the Road . . . to Patterson's Ck. is Hilly down the Ck. on which is good Land, Sloppy to Parker's, and from Parker's to Turner's Hilly again.

Smyth:

I croſſed May's Creek, and Wills's Creek, . . . paſſed by old Fort Cumberland, which is in a beautiful and romantic ſituation, on the north ſide of the Potomack, amidſt vaſt mountains and mighty torrents of water, that break through the mountains in dreadful and tremendous chaſms. . . .

Here I began to aſcend the mighty Alleghany, and . . . after having . . . waded through a black and diſmal river named Savage River, and a number of large and dangerous water-courſes beſides, I arrived at Gregg's habitation, in the midſt of the mountain; where I remained all night amidſt the dreadful

ſcreamings and howlings of multitudes of every ſpecies of wild
beaſts.

---

The emigration from Tidewater westward began in the early part of
the eighteenth century. "The meaner sort of the people (in whom
consists the strength of all Countrys), are daily moving higher up."

1724 or 1725, a 535-acre grant was taken by one William Hawlin
"above Goose Creek on Potowmack river side"—"below the Yaller
rocks"—"on both sides Red Rock Run." Later, Hawlin's widow
took up a grant of 416 acres "about two miles below the Kitchen
Mountain."

And Samuel Skinker took up 672 acres on the south side of Pignut.

---

1753, a group of Moravian brethren journeyed from Pennsylvania
to North Carolina:

> *Oct. 15.* We started at 2:30 A.M. had moonlight and a good
> road. . . . We had a little work done on our wagon, as the pole
> had been injured. The smith charged a big price and his work
> did little good. We saw the Blue Mts. some 8 to 10 miles to our
> right, and had unusually fine weather. We stopped for noon
> eight miles further on by the Kanikatschik. . . . A couple of
> miles beyond we stopped for the night by Corrnell Chimper-
> sen's mill, where we had good water. Br. Nathanael held the
> evening service.
> *Oct. 16.* Br. Grube conducted morning prayers, and we set
> out at 4 A.M. On the way we bought 10 bushels of oats, and
> after driving five miles had breakfast by a creek where Irish
> people live. Two miles further we found good water, also three
> miles beyond, where a house stands back a little on the left. One
> mile brought us to a Tavern. We could again see the Blue Mts.
> quite plainly. In another mile we reached a German inn, where
> we bought some hay and spent the noon hour. Two miles from
> the inn we passed the boundary between Pennsylvania and

Maryland, it is said that Maryland is here only six miles wide. From the Susquehannah here the residents are chiefly Irish, and they have good lands, but one can buy little or nothing from them. Two and a half miles further we came to an old Swiss, where we bought some hay. He was very friendly and asked that we come to see him again. One mile beyond we bought some kraut from a German named Fende'Kra, which tasted very good to us. We went on and camped for the night two miles from the Patomik, putting up our tent by a creek. The man on whose land we were came to see us, was very friendly, and took supper with us. . . . Br. Gottlob held the evening service. . . .

*Oct. 17.* We started at five o'clock and had two miles to go to the Patomik which we reached at daybreak. Br. Jac. Lösch rode in first to find the ford which makes a decided curve between the banks. We crossed safely but it was very difficult to drive out at the other end and we had a great deal of trouble to get up the bank. The river . . . in flood . . . runs far over the high banks, and flows swiftly,—toward the south-east. . . . For supper we cooked chicken, which tasted very good. Br. Nathanael conducted evening prayer.

*Oct. 18.* . . . We turned our horses out to graze in a meadow as we had no feed for them. . . . Br. Gottlob held evening prayers . . . we sang several sweet verses of blessing. . . . Then we lay peacefully down to rest under our tent.

*Oct. 19.* . . . We had a good trip to-day; we could plainly see the Blue Mountains on our right. Some high mountains were directly in front of us. Br. Nathanael held the evening service, and then we went to sleep.

*Oct. 20.* Very early the Brn. brought in our horses from pasture. Br. Grube waked the other Brn. by singing a few verses, and after eating our broth we set out about five o'clock. . . . We traveled eight miles this afternoon, and put up our tent near the Shanidore Creek. . . . We had a pretty camping place tonight, and felt happy, and thankful to the Lord for bringing us safely so far. Br. Nathanael held evening prayers.

Meshach Browning settled in western Maryland:

October being the beginning of the hunting season, my uncle commenced his task of laying in the winter's provisions: some days he would hunt deer, other days for bees; and, as he was most successful in bee-hunting, he spent more of his time in hunting bees than he did in pursuing the deer. Soon our table was abundantly supplied with venison and honey; and the high, fresh tame grass caused our cows to give large quantities of milk, from which aunt, who was a very industrious woman, made plenty of butter; and frequently a fat turkey being added to our table store, we began to think that there was not such a place to be found in all creation. . . .

I kept my stand perhaps five or six minutes, when I saw something slipping through the bushes, which I took to be one of the deer; but I soon found that it was coming toward me. I kept a close look out of it; and directly, within ten steps of me, up rose the head and shoulders of the largest panther that I ever saw, either before or since. . . . I aimed my rifle at him as well as I could, he looking me full in the face; and when I fired he made a tremendous spring for me, and ran off through the brush and briers with the dog after him.

As soon as I recovered a little from my fright, I loaded again and started after them. I followed them as fast as I could, and soon found them at the foot of a large and very high rock; the panther, in his hurry, having sprung down the cleft of rock fifteen or twenty feet; but the dog, being afraid to venture so great a leap, ran around, and the two had met in a thick laurel swamp, where they were fighting the best way they could. . . . I stood on top of the rock over them, and fired at the base of the panther's ear, when down he went; and I ran round the rock. . . . But when I got near him I found he was up and fighting again, and consequently I had to hurry back for my gun, load it again, creep slyly up, take aim at his ear, as before, and give him another shot, which laid him dead on the ground. My first shot had broken his shoulder; the second pierced his ear, passing downward through his tongue; the last entered one ear, and came out the other, scattering his brains all around. He measured eleven feet three inches from the end of his nose to the tip of his tail. This was the largest panther I ever killed. . . .

Mary and myself proposed to walk a little through the beautiful glade, which was covered with grass knee-high, and intermixed with wild flowers of all the kinds and colors that nature had ever produced. All that fancy could desire was here to be seen at a single glance.

. . . A fine snow fell, when off I started again to hunt bears. I saw several tracks, but took the largest one, which I followed rapidly, as the snow was still falling fast; and I had every advantage of the bear, for he could neither hear nor see me. I pushed on after him, until I arrived at a small branch, which the bear was compelled to cross, and in which he had stopped to take a drink. The bank was very high, I did not see him till he bounded up the opposite side into the thick bushes. I could not get a good sight of him till he was at some distance; but knowing that would be my last chance, as he reached the top of the hill, I fired at him, hit or miss. I reloaded my gun, and went to where I last saw him, when I discovered he was badly wounded, there being a great quantity of blood along his trail.

. . . The bear was obliged to retreat about a mile through cleared ground, where I could not only run as fast, if not faster than him, but also where I had a fair chance for a hand-to-hand fight. I followed the trail, running with all my might. Observing him making all the head-way he could, I increased my speed till within gun-shot, when I fired at him a second time; but seeing no change in his speed, I loaded as I ran, in order to lose no ground and, coming still closer to him, I gave him a third shot. Still, on he went; but as I saw he was failing, I loaded again as I ran, and poured in a fourth fire, which I found made him stagger considerably in his gait. I then saw that one of his thighs was broken. By this time he had entered a small ravine, having steep banks on each side, where I could run round and head him off; in doing which, I saw a large tree laying across the branch he was traveling up. I went out on this log till I got about the middle of the branch, where I stood, unseen by the bear, till he was almost under me, when I notified him that I was there, by saying, 'Old fellow, you are mine at last.' He stopped to see what was the matter, when I took the fifth shot at his head, and down he went into the water. In the twinkling of an eye I sprang from the log, knowing that I could cut his throat before he recovered from the effect of the shot. I seized him by the ear, and holding his head up, I slashed his neck through to the bone, and from ear to ear, in a couple of cuts.

. . . The dogs started off in full cry after what we were pretty certain was a bear, and in a short time we heard the fighting begin. The dogs would run awhile, and fight awhile; and after a chase of at least three miles, all the time coming nearer home, the bear at last ran into a large glade, in full view of Colonel Lynn's house. It so happened that General Lee, . . . who fought with General Washington, was on his road to the West, and had stopped with Colonel Lynn a few days. When the dogs and the bear came in sight, the whole family, together with General Lee, came out to see the sport. Hugh and I came into the glade, and commenced hostilities at once; and after three rounds fired at him, the bear yielded to superior numbers, there being four to one; and he died like a hero, fighting till the last breath left him.

I turned to follow the dog; but all again becoming quiet, I listened with anxiety, when I heard something moving behind me. I looked around, and beheld the panther coming toward me, but not near enough for me to shoot. He made a short turn, which brought him opposite me, and within ten steps; but he went on the off side of a rock, that covered him from my shot. As I saw he would have to come from behind the rock, and be exposed to my view, I held my fire till he came out; and as soon as he made his appearance, I let him have a shot, which I directed as near as I could for his heart. As the gun cracked he sprang into the air, snapping at the place where the ball had struck him; and then turning towards me, he came on till within about five steps of me, put his paws on a small fallen tree, and looked me full in

the face. While he stood looking at me, I saw the blood stream-
ing from both sides of his body. . . .

As I went on, walking fast, I came to some shelly rocks, where
the snakes began to rattle; the weeds seemed to be shaking all
around me, and I could see them twisting themselves in every
direction. . . .

I then followed the trail, with great difficulty, till it became
fresher; when off went the dogs, and immediately they were on
the old fellow in a hollow tree; and such fighting, and cutting
with teeth, I never saw before or since. He was the largest and
strongest wolf I ever met in my life. He remained in the tree,
with his mouth wide open; and every time a dog came within
reach, he would sink every tooth into him. I encouraged the
dogs to make another set at him; when the strongest took a deep
hold on one of the wolf ears, while the other seized the remaining one. He then bounded from the tree, and the two dogs
threw him on the ground. He tried again and again to recover
his feet, but they tumbled him down, until they were all tired;
when I took a club and beat him on the head until he was dead. I
took off his scalp and hide, which were worth nine dollars. . . .

I was once making wild Hay in a glade . . .

In the morning, when I saw such a beautiful snow on the
ground, I told Mr. Little that I would try to find where the old
panther had her residence. . . . I had not made more than half
my circuit, when I found her track, where she had come out of
a swamp and was taking a straight course for the Savage river,
which ran through a very mountainous country, covered with
almost impenetrable thickets.

Traveling on with a light foot and willing mind, I presently
found a fine large doe, which she had killed, and sucked its
blood. The body being still warm, I skinned it, took the track
again, and followed it over the Meadow Mountain down to the
Savage river, and on to the steep hills along its border. . . .

When I got my eyes on her, she was looking me in the face, and distant not more than five steps. I took careful aim between her eyes, let her have the whole load in her brains, and down she dropped, without scarcely making a struggle. I skinned and scalped her. . . .

All the settlers lived in cabins, and fed their children on bread, meat, butter, honey, and milk; coffee and tea were almost out of the question, being only used by a very few old ladies who had been raised in other parts of the country. . . .

Hellebore is the first weed that shoots up in the spring, and it grows to the height of two feet, with a stalk somewhat resembling that of corn, and a strong, broad leaf. It grows in marshy ground and this place, being a narrow, muddy branch, was full of it. The bear had got into the mud, and was amusing himself by biting off the hellebores and slinging them out of his way.

This he continued to do until I was on the bank of the run, and within thirty steps of him. I then knew that he was my prize, and I stood quietly looking at him playing; for I had never before seen a grown bear play. . . .

Seeing that he [the bear] was still biting the dog severely, and that I could effect nothing with the knife, I ran up suddenly, seized him by the wool on his hips, and gave him a hard jerk, which as he was very weak, threw him flat on the ground. He then gave a long groan, which was so much like that of a human being, that it made me feel as though I had been dealing foully with the beast; but there I had to stand, and hear his heavy groans, which no person could have distinguished from those of a strong man in the last agonies of death.

I stood looking calmly at him, until the sport was marred by the thought of the brave manner in which he had defended himself against such unequal numbers, and it really seemed to me that I had committed a crime against an unoffending animal.

In 1803, a book was published:

A
TREATISE
on
PRACTICAL FARMING;
EMBRACING PARTICULARLY
THE FOLLOWING SUBJECTS, VIZ.

The USE of PLAISTER of PARIS, with Directions
for Using it; and GENERAL OBSERVATIONS
on the USE of OTHER MANURES.

ON DEEP PLOUGHING; THICK SOWING of
GRAIN; METHOD OF PREVENTING FRUIT
TREES from DECAYING, and

Farming in General.

BY JOHN A. BINNS,
OF LOUDON COUNTY, VIRGINIA, FARMER

FREDERICK-TOWN, MARIAND,
Printed by JOHN B. COLVIN - Editor of
the REPUBLICAN ADVOCATE.
1803

Binns's "plaister of paris" was actually gypsum, and its use revolu-
tionized Piedmont agriculture. Jefferson: "The county of Loudon
. . . had been so exhausted and wasted by bad husbandry that it
began to depopulate, the inhabitants going Southwardly in quest of
better lands. . . . It is now become one of the most productive
Counties of the State of Virginia and the price given for the lands is
multiplied manifold."

In the Piedmont and in the naturally fertile Shenandoah Valley,
German settlers from Pennsylvania established small arms—50 to
100 acres, planted grasses, fenced and housed their stock, introduced

a varied family husbandry, and quickly became richer than the land-poor Tidewater colonists.

Burnaby, on the Shenandoah Germans:

> I could not but reflect with pleasure on the situation of these people: and think if there is such a thing as happiness in this life, that they enjoy it. Far from the bustle of the world, they live in the most delightful climate, and richest soil imaginable; they are everywhere surrounded with beautiful prospects and sylvan scenes; lofty mountains, transparent streams, falls of water, rich valleys, and majestic woods; the whole interspersed with an infinite variety of flowering shrubs, constitute the landscape surrounding them: they are subject to few diseases; are generally robust; and live in perfect liberty: they are ignorant of want.

Captain Ferdinand Marie Bayard, writing in 1791:

> It is a magnificent country about Winchester. The men are tall, well-made, of strong constitutions, and ruddy. The horses and cattle have the eye and the gait of health.

---

Smyth:

> Many of the Irish here can ſcarcely ſpeak in English and thouſands of the Germans underſtand no language but High Dutch however they are all very laborious, and extremely induſtrious, having improved this part of the country beyond conception; but they have no idea of ſocial life, and are more like brutes than men.

And Kercheval:

> There was soon a mixed population of Germans, Irish, and a few English and Scotch. The national prejudices which existed between the Dutch and Irish produced much disorder and many riots. It was customary for the Dutch, on St. Patrick's Day, to

exhibit the effigy of the saint, with a string of Irish potatoes around his neck.

———————

The fenfible, and this I flatter myfelf, is the greater part of this nation, feem to be fully perfuaded, that it is impoffible for a country to flourifh and become powerful, without country Manufactures. . . .

I know by experience, that one of the wifeft Princes now in Europe preferred a plain but induftrious Manufacturer at his Levee, fpoke with him above an hour, when at the fame time, he did not look at a number of the greateft and richeft of the Nobility of his dominions, whofe principal occupation is to opprefs their farmers and hunt foxes. . . .

I have purchafed an advantageoufly fituated tract of land on Patowmack, not far from the mouth of Monocafy, of two thousand one hundred acres, which except a fmall balance, is paid—on this land I have erected all the neceffary buildings for the Manufactory, as glafs ovens for bottles, window and flint glafs, and a dwelling houfe for one hundred and thirty-five now living fouls—I have made a beginning of glafs making.

Johann Friedrich Amelung, German glass-maker of New Bremen, who purchased 2100 acres north and east of Sugarloaf Mountain, later added another 900 acres. Some of his land purchases were as follows:

| | | |
|---|---|---|
| Part of Gantt's Garden ....... | 1570 | acres |
| Adam's Bones............... | 194 | " |
| Tobacco Hook.............. | 71 | " |
| I Don't Care What .......... | 51 | " |

Amelung raised money in Germany and America, and with sixty-eight trained glass workers, their families, a pastor, and two teachers, as well as a few other tradesmen, sailed from Bremen in June, 1784.

Within two years, he spent more money than he had raised. Congress refused him a loan.

The real reason for Amelung's failure was probably the fact that he could not adjust himself to the demands of the new country. He had high-flown, artistic notions; he apparently wanted to produce artistic glass products in the style of the Venetian and Bohemian glass blowers and realized too late that the time for this sort of thing had not yet arrived in America. The country needed window-panes and medicine bottles, not delicate wine glasses and flower vases.

Jefferson:

The passage of the Potomac through the Blue Ridge is, perhaps, one of the most stupendous scenes in nature. You stand on a very high point of land. On your right comes up the Shenandoah, having ranged along the foot of the mountain an hundred miles to seek a vent. On your left approaches the Potomac, in quest of a passage also. In the moment of their junction, they rush together against the mountain, rend it asunder, and pass off to the sea. The first glance of this scene hurries our senses into the opinion, that this earth has been created in time, that the mountains were formed first, that the rivers began to flow afterwards, that in this place particularly, they have been dammed up by the Blue Ridge of Mountains, and have formed an ocean which filled the whole valley; that continuing to rise they have at length broken over at this spot, and have torn the mountain down from its summit to its base. The piles of rock on each hand, but particularly the Shenandoah, the evident marks of their disrupture and avulsion from their beds by the most powerful agents of nature, corroborate the impression. But the distant finishing which nature has given to the picture, is of a very different character. It is a true contrast to the foreground. It is as placid and delightful as that is wild and tremendous. For the mountain being cloven asunder, she presents to your eye, through the cleft, a small catch of smooth blue horizon, at an infinite distance in the plain country, inviting you, as it were, from the riot and tumult roaring around, to pass through the breach and participate of the calm below. Here the eye ultimately composes itself; and that way, too, the road happens actually to lead. You cross the Potomac above the junction, pass along its side through the base of the mountain for three miles, its terrible precipices hanging in fragments over you, and within about twenty miles reach Fredericktown, and the fine country round that. This scene is worth a voyage across the Atlantic.

⟨geology⟩

*A geological section of the State of Maryland, from the top of Savage Mountain to Point Lookout at the mouth of the Potomac, exhibits in miniature a section of the geology of the world, from the most recent tertiary deposits to the most ancient rock formations. Penetrating this area, the Potomac flows through the five distinct physiographic regions of the eastern seaboard: the Allegheny Plateau, the Ridge and Valley Province, the Blue Ridge, the Piedmont and the Coastal Plain—each with its characteristic geology, terrain and forest cover. Headwaters originate in the first three of these regions; only one major tributary—the Mono-cacy— rises in the Piedmont Plateau.*

*A heavily dissected peneplain, the Allegheny Plateau is composed of nearly flat-lying carboniferous rocks—the coal country—and is bounded on the southeast by the Allegheny Front or Allegheny Escarpment. Southeastward lies the Ridge and Valley Province, fifty to sixty miles wide: this is the Valley, the Great Valley, the Hagerstown Valley (Maryland), the Cumberland Valley (Pennsylvania), the Shenandoah Valley, the Valley of Virginia. Bounded on either side by an abrupt scarp of shales and sandstones, the valley floor is generally level or gently rolling, and consists largely of decomposed limestones. It is intensely fertile, and the soft limestone is honeycombed with caverns. Some of the oldest rocks known on earth—of Archeozoic and Lower Cambrian times—are the granitic gneisses occasionally exposed in the Blue Ridge Province, notably in the banks and islands of the Potomac River, and on the Ridge itself (as Old Rag Granite). Antietam quartzite and Harper's shale are similarly ancient. Now a large uphold of crystalline rocks, dipping in parts beneath the Valley, the Ridge was formed originally deep beneath the surface, as molten lava. A major fault probably extends along its full length. Litho-logically akin to the Blue Ridge in its western areas is the Piedmont Province, composed of granites, gneisses and schists, greenstone, soap-stone, and marble, creating a heavy, fertile soil. Like the Blue Ridge, the grain or strike of the Piedmont is from northeast to southwest. In its lower areas, toward the southeast, it is covered in places by an outwash deposit of gravel and sand, spread by the Potomac, and here the materials of the Piedmont have been so altered that their original structures and evidences of origin have been obliterated. Southeasternmost, where the Potomac becomes a tidal estuary, lies the Coastal Plain—beginning roughly at the Great Falls, and extending to Chesapeake Bay and beyond, one hundred miles beneath the surface of the Atlantic Ocean. Composed of clays, sandstones, greensands, shell marl, coarse and cobbly gravels, formed by the washing down of soil and rocky debris from crystalline Piedmont rocks (on whose eastward continuation the material is superimposed), the Coastal Plain dips gently seaward. The boundary between Piedmont and Plain is best defined at Great Falls and the Palisades, where the Potomac leaves the last of the upland rock. Elsewhere, across the land it is a sinuous and ill-defined border, the softer Plain formations feathering out as they lap onto the obdurate crystalline rocks.*

# Federal City

George Washington, 1790:

July
Monday, 12th. Exercised on Horseback between 5 and 6 in the
morning.
   Sat for Mr. Trumbull from 9 until half after ten. And about
Noon had two Bills presented to me by the joint Committee of
Congress—The one 'An Act for Establishing the Temporary
and permanent Seat. . . '

An Act for establishing the temporary and permanent seat of
the Government of the United States

SECTION 1. *Be it enacted by the Senate and House of Representatives
of the United States of America in Congress assembled,* That a
district of territory, not exceeding ten miles square, to be located
as hereafter directed on the river Potomac, at some place between
the mouths of the Eastern Branch [Anacostia River] and Con-
nogochegue, be, and the same is hereby, accepted for the permanent seat of the government of the United States.

Washington considered various sites: the vicinity of the Conococheague . . . at the mouth of the Monocacy . . . in the Georgetown
area . . .

Georgetown property owners offered their land: "It is conceived that
the hilliness of the country, far from being an objection, will be
thought a desirable circumstance, as it will at once contribute to the
beauty, health and security of a city intended for the seat of Empire.
For a place merely commercial, where men willingly sacrifice health
to gain, a continued flat might perhaps be preferred."

The location was chosen, and Washington wrote from Philadelphia, February 3, 1791, to William Deakins, Jr., and Benjamin Stoddert:

> Gentlemen: In asking your aid in the following case permit me at the same time to ask the most perfect secrecy.
>
> The federal territory being located, the competition for the location of the town now rests between the mouth of the Eastern branch, and the land on the river, below and adjacent to George-town. In favour of the former, Nature has furnished powerful advantages. In favour of the latter is its vicinity to Georgetown, which puts it in the way of deriving aids from it in the beginning, and of communicating in return an increased value to the property of that town. These advantages have been so poised in my mind as to give it different tendencies at different times. There are lands which stand yet in the way of the latter location and which, if they would be obtained, for the purposes of the town, would remove a considerable obstacle to it, and go near indeed to decide what has been so long on the balance with me. . . .
>
> The object of this letter is to ask you to endeavor to purchase these grounds of the owners for the public . . . but as if for yourselves, and to conduct your propositions so as to excite no suspicion that they are on behalf of the public.

Later—December 1791—Washington wrote:

> Potomac River then, is the centre of the Union. It is between the extremes of heat and cold. It is not so far to the south as to be unfriendly to grass, nor so far north as to have the produce of the Summer consumed in the length, and severity of the winter. It waters that soil, and runs in that climate, which is most congenial to English grains, and most agreeable to the Cultivators of them.
>
> It is the River, more than any other, in my opinion, which must, in the natural progress of things, connect by its inland navigation . . . the Atlantic States with the vast region which is populating (beyond all conception) to the Westward of it. It is

designated by law for the seat of Empire; and must, from its extensive course through a rich and populous country become, in time, the grand Emporium of North America. To these reasons may be added that, the lands within, and surrounding the district of Columbia are as high, as dry, and as healthy as any in the United States.

And Tobias Lear, 1793:

The whole area of the City consists of upwards of four thousand acres.—The ground, on an average, is about forty feet above the water of the river. Although the whole, when taken to-gether, appears to be nearly a level spit, yet it is found to consist of what may be called wavy land; and is sufficiently uneven to give many very extensive and beautiful views from various parts of it, as well as to effectually answer every purpose of cleansing and draining the city.

---

Thomas Jefferson would have preferred a site near the Great Falls, for, among other reasons, "remoteness from the influence of any overgrown commercial city." However, he accepted the site chosen:

*November 29, 1790*
*Proceedings to be had under the Residence act.*
a territory not exceeding 10. miles square (or, I presume, 100 square miles in any form) to be located by metes and bounds.
    3. commissioners to be appointed
       I suppose them not entitled to salary.
the Commissioners to purchase or accept 'such quantity of land on the E. side of the river as the President shall deem *proper for the U.S.*' viz. for the federal Capitol, the offices, the President's house & gardens, the town house, Market house, publick walls, hospital. . . .
    The Comissioners should have some taste in architecture, because they may have to decide between different plans.
    They will however be subject to the President's direction in every point.

He wrote on January 29, 1791:

The President having thought Major L'Enfant peculiarly quali-
fied to make such a draught of the ground as will enable himself
to fix on the spot for the public buildings, he has been written to
for that purpose.

Major of Engineers Pierre Charles L'Enfant enjoyed the unofficial
position of Advisor in Aesthetics to the new government. "When-
ever, during the war or after, something in any way connected with
art was wanted, L'Enfant was as a matter of course appealed to." He
relieved the monotony at Valley Forge with his quick pencil sketches,
and even Washington sat for his likeness to be drawn by the man he
called "Monsieur Langfang."

It was said of L'Enfant that he always saw things "en grande."

Jefferson to L'Enfant, March 1791:

*Sir,* You are desired to proceed to Georgetown, where you will
find Mr. Ellicott employed in making a survey and map of the
Federal territory. The special object of asking your aid is to have
drawings of the particular grounds most likely to be approved
for the site of the federal town and buildings. You will therefore
be pleased to begin on the eastern branch, and proceed from
thence upwards, laying down the hills, valleys, morasses, and
waters between that, the Potomac, the Tyber, and the road
leading from Georgetown to the eastern branch, and connecting the whole with certain fixed points of the map Mr. Ellicott
is preparing. Some idea of the height of the hills above the base
on which they stand, would be desirable.

From the *Georgetown Weekly Ledger,* March 12, 1791:

Some time last month arrived in this town Maj. Andrew Ellicott, a gentleman of superior astronomical abilities. He was
appointed by the President of the United States to lay off a tract
of land ten miles square on the Potomac for the use of Congress.

He is now engaged in this business and hopes soon to accomplish the object of his mission. He is attended by Benjamin Banniker, an Ethiopian. . . .
Wednesday evening arrived in this town Major Longfont.

Washington's notes for the federal city:

Quary Stone to be raised by Skilful People.
The buildings, especially the Capitol, ought to be on a scale far superior to any thing in *this* Country; the House for the President should also (in the design though not executed all at once) be upon a Commensurate scale.

Washington to the secretary of state, March 31, 1791:

The terms agreed on between me, on the part of the United States, with the Land holders of Georgetown and Carrollsburg are. That all the land from Rock Creek along the river to the Eastern-branch and so upwards to or above the Ferry including a breadth of about a mile and a half, the whole containing from three to five thousand acres, is ceded to the public, on condition That, when the whole shall be surveyed and laid off as a city, (which Major L'Enfant is now directed to do) the present Proprietors shall retain every other lot; and, for such part of the land as may be taken for public use for squares, walks, &ca., they shall be allowed at the rate of Twenty five pounds per acre. The Public having the right to reserve such parts of the wood on the land as may be thought necessary to be preserved for ornament &ca. The Land holders to have the use and profits of all their ground until the city is laid off into lots, and sale is made of those lots which, by this agreement, become public property. No compensation is to be made for the ground that may be occupied as streets or alleys.

Washington's diary, June 1791:

Tuesday, 28th. Whilst the Commissioners were engaged in preparing the Deed to be signed by the Subscribers this afternoon, I went out with Majr. L'Enfant and Mr. Ellicot to take a more perfect view of the ground, in order to decide finally on the spots on which to place the public buildings and to direct how a line which was to leave out a Spring (commonly known by the name of the Cool Spring) belonging to Majr. Stoddart should be run.

And July 20, 1791:

> I am now happy to add that all matters between the Proprietors of the soil and the public are settled to the mutual satisfaction of the Parties, and that the business of laying out the city, the grounds for public buildings, walks &c. is progressing under the inspection of Major L'Enfant with pleasing prospects.

---

L'Enfant to Washington, September 1789:

> Ser;
> The late determination of Congress to lay the foundation of a city which is to become the Capital of this vast Empire offers so great an occasion. . . .
> No nation, perhaps, had ever before the opportunity offered them of deliberately deciding on the spot where their Capital City should be fixed. . . . And, although the means now within the power of the Country are not such as to pursue the design to any great extent, it will be obvious that the plans should be drawn on such a scale as to leave room for that aggrandizement and embellishment which the increase of the wealth of the nation will permit it to pursue at any period, however remote.

To Hamilton:

> I feel a sort of embarrassment how to speak to you as advantageously as I really think of the situation determined upon. I become apprehensive of being charged with partiality when I assure you that no position in America can be more susceptible of grand improvement.

To Jefferson, Georgetown, March 11, 1791:

*Sir:*
I have the honor of informing you of my arrival at this place
where I could not possibly reach before Wednesday last and
very late in the evening after having travelled part of the way on
foot and part on horse back leaving the broken stage behind.

On arriving I made it my first care immediately to wait on
the mayor of the town in conforming with the direction which
you gave me—he appeared to be much surprised and assured
me he had received no previous notice of my coming nor any
instruction relating to the business I was sent upon. . . . I am
only at present to regret that an heavy rain and thick mist which
has been incessant ever since my arrival here has put an insuper-
able obstacle to my wish of proceeding immediately to the
survey. Should the weather continue bad as there is every
appearance it will I shall be much at a loss how to make a plan of
the ground you have pointed out to me and have it ready for the
President at the time when he is expected at this place. I see no
other way if by Monday next the weather does not change, but
that of making a rough draft as accurate as may be obtained by
viewing the ground in riding over it on horse back, as I have
already done yesterday through the rain to obtain a knowledge
of the whole. I put from the eastern branch towards Georgetown up the heights and down along side of the bank of the main
river and along side of Goose and Rock creeks as far up as their
springs.

As far as I was able to judge through a thick fog I passed on
many spots which appeared to me raly beautiful and which
seem to dispute with each other who command. In the most
extensive prospect of the water the gradual rising of the ground
from Carrollborough toward the Ferry Road, the level and
extensive ground from there to the bank of the Potomack as far
as Goose Creek present a situation most advantageous to run
streets and prolong them on grand and far distant point of view
the water running from spring at some distance into the creeks,
appeared also to me possible to be conducted without much

labour so as to form pounds for watering every part of that spot. . . .

No proof of the ground between the eastern branch and Georgetown can be say to be of a commanding nature, on the contrary it appear to first sight as being itself surrounded, however in advancing toward the eastern branch these heights seem to sink as the waves of a tempestuous sea.

L'Enfant to Jefferson:

jeorgetown april the 4th. 1791

*Sir.*

. . . ·The number and nature of the publick building with the necessary appendix I should be glad to have a statement of as speedily as possible—and I would be very much obliged to you in the meantime if you could procure for me what Ever may fall within your reach—of any of the different grand city now existing such as for example—as London—madry—paris —Amsterdam—naples—venice—genoa—florence together with particular maps. . . . For notwithstanding I would reprobate the Idea of Imitating and that contrary of Having this Intention it is my wish and shall be my Endeavor to delineate on a new and original way the plan the contrivance of which the President has left to me without any restriction soever—yet the contemplation of what exist of well improved situation, given the parallel of these, with deffective ones, may serve to suggest a variety of new Ideas and is necessary to refine and strengthen the Judgement.

From L'Enfant's notes:

. . . there were the level ground on the water and all round were it decend but most particularly on that part terminating in a ridge to Jenkins Hill and running in a paralell with at half mile off from the river Potowmack separated by a low ground intersected with three grand streams—many of the most desirable position offer for to Erect the Publique Edifices thereon— from these height every grand building would rear with a majestied aspect over the Country all around and might be advantageously seen from twenty miles off which Contiguous to the first setlement of the City they would there stand to ages in a Central point to it, facing on the grandest prospect of both branch of the Potowmack with the town of Alexandry in front seen in its fullest extend over many points of land projecting from the Mariland and Virginia shore in a manner as add much to the perspective. . . .

Thus in every respect advantageously situated, the Federal City would soon grow of itself and spread as the branches of a tree do. . . .

After much menutial search for an elligible situation, prompted I may say from a fear of being prejudiced in favour of a first opinion I could discover no one so advantageously to greet the congressional building as is that on the west end of Jenkins heights which stand as a pedastal waiting for a monument, and I am confidant, were all the wood cleared from the ground no situation could stand in competition with this. . . .

It is not the regular assemblage of houses laid out in square and forming streets all parrallel and uniform that is so necessary for such plan could only do on a well level plain and were no surrounding object being interesting it become indifferent which way the opening of street may be directed.

but on any other ground a plan of this sort must be defective and it never would answer for any of the spots proposed for the Federal City, and on that held here as the most eligible it would absolutely annihilate every advantage enumerated and the seeing of which will alone injure the success of the undertaking.

such regular plan indeed however answerable as they may appear upon paper or seducing as they may be on the first aspect to the eyes of some people most even when applyed upon the ground the best calculated to admit of it become at last tiresome and insipide and it never could be in its orrigine but a mean continuance of some cool imagination wanting a sense of the real grand and truly beautifull only to be met with were nature contribut with art and diversify the objects.

having first determined some principal points to which I wished making the rest subordinate I next made the distribution regular with the streets at right angle *north-south* and *east west* but afterwards I opened others on various directions as avenues to and from every principal places, wishing by this not merely to contrast with the general regularity nor to afford a greater variety of pleasant seats and prospect as will be obtained from the advantageous ground over the which the avenues are mostly directed but principally to connect each part of the city with more efficacy by, if I may so express, making the real distance less from place to place in managing on them a resiprocity of sight. . . .

[t]hose avenues which will afford a variety of pleasant rides, and become the means for a rapid intercourse with all parts of the city, to which they will serve as does the main artery in the animal body. . . .

A fall which issuing from under the base of the Congress building may there form a cascade of forty feet heigh or more than one hundred wide which would produce the most happy effect in rolling down to fill up the canall and discharge itself in the Potowmack of which it would then appear as the main spring when seen through that grand and majestic avenue intersecting with the prospect from the palace. . . .

. . . to procure to the palace and all other houses from that place to congress a prospect of the Potowmack the which will acquire new swiftness being laid over the green of a field well level and made brilliant by shade of few trees artfully planted.

---

L'Enfant prepared a map of his plan, but he refused to release it to the Commissioners, who wished to proceed with the sale of lots. L'Enfant feared that they only wanted to accommodate speculators and were not anxious to cooperate in establishing his plan. The Commissioners complained to Washington, who replied:

> It is much to be regretted, however common the case is, that men who possess talents which fit them for peculiar purposes should almost invariably be under the influence of an untoward disposition or are sottish idle, or possessed of some other disqualification by which they plague all those with whom they are concerned. But I did not expect to have met with such perverseness in Major L'Enfant as his late conduct exhibited. . . .
>
> I have no other motive . . . than merely to shew that the feelings of such Men are always alive, and, where their assistance is essential; that it is policy to humour them or to put on the appearance of doing it.

But L'Enfant held onto the map—for a while.

In the fall of 1791, Mr. Daniel Carroll, prominent local citizen and a relative of one of the Commissioners, started to build a house across one of L'Enfant's surveying lines. L'Enfant warned him that, if the house were built, he would order it taken down. Construction continued.

L'Enfant to the Commissioners, November 21:

> Respecting the house of Mr. Carroll of Duddington . . . I directed yesterday forenoon a number of hands to the spot and employed with them some of the principal people who had worked in raising the house to the end that every possible attention be paid to the interests of the gentleman as shall be consistent in forwarding the public object.
>
> The roof is already down with part of the brickwork and the whole will I expect be leveled to the ground before the week is over.

Commissioners to Washington, November 25:

> We are sorry to be under the disagreeable necessity of mention-
> ing to you an occurance which must wound your feelings. On
> our meeting here today, we were to our great astonishment
> informed that, Maj.ʳ L'Enfant, without any Authority from us,
> & without even having submitted to our consideration, has
> proceeded to demolish, M.ʳ Carroll's house. M.ʳ Carroll who
> had received some letters from the Maj.ʳ on the subject, fearing
> the consequences obtained an injunction from the Chancellor,
> for him to desist; with a summons to Maj.ʳ L'Enfant to attend the
> Court of Chancery in December, to receive his decision on the
> subject, but before his return the house was in part demol-
> ished. . . . Anticipating your feelings on this subject, and fully
> apprised of the Maj.ʳˢ fitness for the work he is employed in, we
> cannot forbear expressing a hope that the affair may be still so
> adjusted that we may not Lose his services.

Commissioners to L'Enfant, November 26:

> On our meeting this day were equally surprised and concerned
> to find that you had proceeded to demolish Mr. Carroll's house.
> We were impelled by many considerations to give immediate
> directions to those acting in your absence to desist. . . . Our
> opinion ought to have been previously taken on a subject so
> delicate and so interesting.

Washington wrote to Jefferson, November 30, requesting that he

> Judge from the complexion of things how far [L'Enfant] may be
> spoken to in decisive terms without losing his services; which,
> in my opinion would be a serious misfortune.—At the same
> time, *he must know,* there is a line beyond which he will not be
> suffered to go.

Jefferson to L'Enfant, December 1:

> I have received with sincere concern the information from
> yourself as well as others, that you proceeded to demolish the
> house of m͞r Carrol of Duddington, against his consent, and
> without authority from the Commissioners, or any other per-
> son. in this you have laid yourself open to the laws, & in a
> country where they will have their course, to their animadver-
> sion will belong the present case.—in future I must strictly
> enjoin you to touch no man's property, without his consent, or
> the previous order of the Commissioners. I wished you to be
> employed in the arrangements of the federal city. I still wish it:
> but only on condition that you can conduct yourself in subor-
> dination to the authority of the Commissioners, to the laws of
> the land, & to the rights of it's citizens.

L'Enfant appealed to the Commissioners:

> He erected that House on ground he knew was not his . . . and
> that it was questionable when he proceeded to build if the whole
> Spote he possessed himself of should not be thus appropriated.

Commissioners to Jefferson, December 8:

> As the house was nearly demolished before the Chancellors
> injunction arrived, Mr. Carroll did not think it worth while to
> have it served, trusting perhaps, that our directions expressly
> forbidding their further proceedings in it would have been
> attended to—We are sorry to mention that the Majr. who was
> absent at the time we issued them, paid no attention to them
> but completely demolished it on his return, this instance has
> given fresh alarm. . . . The Majr. has indeed done us the honour
> of writing us a letter justifying his conduct—We have not
> noticed it.

From Jefferson's notes, December 11:

> I confess, that on a view of L'Enfant's proceedings and letters latterly, I am thoroughly persuaded that, to render him useful, his temper must be subdued.

Washington to L'Enfant, December 13:

> Sir: I have received your letter . . . and can only once more, and now for all, inform you that every matter and thing which has relation to the Federal district, and the City within it, is committed to the Commissioners appointed. . . .
>
> Were it necessary, I would again give it to you as my opinion that the Commissioners have every disposition that can be desired to listen to your suggestions, to adopt your plans, and to support your authority for carrying the latter into effect, as far as it shall appear reasonable, just and prudent to them, and consistent with the powers under which they act themselves. But having said this in more instances than one it is rather painful to reiterate it. With esteem and regard I am etc.

Washington to the Commissioners, December 18:

> His aim is obvious. It is to have as much scope as possible for the display of his talents, perhaps for his ambition. . . . I submit to your consideration whether it might not be politic to give him pretty general, and ample powers for *defined* objects; until you shall discover in him a disposition to abuse them.
>
> His pride would be gratified, and his ambition excited by such a mark of your confidence. If for want of these, or from any other cause he should take amiss and leave the business, I have no scruple in declaring to *you* (though I do not want *him* to know it) that I know not where another is to be found, who could supply his place.

January 18, 1792, Washington to Jefferson:

> The conduct of Majr. L'Enfant and those employed under him, astonishes me beyond measure!

Jefferson to L'Enfant, February 22:

> I am charged by the President to say that your continuance would be desirable to him; & at the same time to add that the law requires it should be in subordination to the Commissioners.

L'Enfant's reply, February 26:

> My desire to conform to the judgement and wishes of the President have really been ardent. and I trust my actions always have manifested those desires more uncontrovertable . . . to change a wilderness into a city, to erect and beautify buildings etc. to that degree of perfection necessary to receive the seat of Government of a vast empire. . . . If there the law absolutely requires without any equivocation that my continuance shall depend upon an appointment from the Commissioners—I cannot nor would I upon any consideration submit myself to it.

Jefferson to L'Enfant, February 27:

> From your letter received yesterday in answer to my last . . . it is understood you absolutely decline acting under the authority of the present Commissioners, if this understanding of your meaning be right, I am instructed by the president to inform you that not withstanding the desire he has entertained to preserve your agency in the business, the condition upon which it is to be done is inadmissable & your services must be at an end.

Jefferson to Daniel Carroll, March 1:

> Much time has been spent in endeavoring to induce Major Lenfant to continue in the business he was engaged in, in proper subordination to the Commissioners. he has however entirely

refused, so that he has been notified that we consider his services as at an end. the plan is put into the hands of an engraver, and will be engraved within three or four weeks.

The Georgetown proprietors, greatly upset, petitioned the President to reconsider. But Washington felt that he, not l'Enfant, had been insulted: "No further overtures will *ever* be made to this Gentn. by the Government."

L'Enfant's plans went into execution, without him.

---

Washington:

> The Plan of the City having met universal applause (as far as my information goes) and Major L'Enfant having become a very discontented man, it was thought that less than from 2500 to 3000 dollars would not be proper to offer him for his services: instead of this, suppose five hundred guineas and a Lot in a good part of the City was to be substituted? I think it would be more pleasing, and less expensive.

The Commissioners officially offered l'Enfant $2,500, which he refused, and remained silent for eight years.

> Washington: "Did Major L'Enfant assign any reason for his rejection of the compensation offered him?"

L'Enfant had started work on the Federal City without contract or other financial agreement. When his plan was published, he received nothing for it, having neglected to copyright it. Starting in 1800, he presented memorials to Congress and the Commissioners; the small sums they voted him were consumed by creditors.

> To the Commissioners of the City of Washington
> PHILADELPHIA *August 30th* 1800
> A concurrence of disastrous events rendering my position so difficult as to be no longer possible to withstand unless speadily relief be obtained by collecting what yet remains my due . . .

He wrote to Jefferson, 1801:

> The peculiarity of my position and the embarrassement ansuing
> from the conduct of the Board of the Commissionaires of the
> City of Washington in regard to requests and communications
> made to them rendering the freedome of a direct address to you
> unavoidable—I hope the necessity will plead my excuse and
> seeing the time near approaches when it is presumable you will
> wish to call Congress attention to the State of things relative to
> this new Seat of Government; I now with great dependence on
> your goodness beg your consideration of the circumstances
> with me.
>       . . . I will no more than express—that I after many heavy
> pecuniary Sacrifices occasioned by variety of Situations during
> the revolution war—I since the peace of 1783 was also differ-
> ently Encouraged and Invited by many Commissions to the
> free spending of my own, dependent upon promises of regular
> reappointment with promotion all which ended to my loss and
> absolut ruin.—that on the particular Instance of my agency to
> the Enterprise of the City of Washington I have received no
> remuneration what ever, that—no kind of preconvention were
> for the Service no price agree upon for plans, nor the Copy right
> conceded to the Commissionaires nor to any ones else, and
> that—extended as was my Concerns and agency beyond the
> usual to Architects; although by the grand Combination of new
> Schems I contributed eminently to the ensurance of the city
> establishment by which numbers of Individuals and the Coun-
> try to an immense distance desire a increasing of their wealth I
> deed by no one opperations nor transactions worked on my
> own profit.
>       Acquainted Ser as you necessarily must have become with
> managements of the City affairs in which my free exertions
> were not the least usefull to the promotion of the national
> object—the merite, and that of orriginating of the plan you,
> doubtless, will readily allow to me and certain I am that—for all
> what I suffered, the only reproach to which I may be liable . . .
> is my having been more faithfull to a principle than ambition—
> too zealous in my pursuits—and too hazardous on a depend-
> ence on mouth friends.

L'Enfant presented to Congress a bill for his services in the amount of $95,000; this was rejected, and he finally accepted the $2,500 originally offered.

Destitute, he was rescued by a friendly planter, Dudley Digges, who took care of him at his country house, Green Hill, near Silver Spring, not far from Clean Drinking Manor.

L'Enfant died in 1825, leaving personal effects valued at $46.

---

Nicholas King, surveyor of the City of Washington, to President Thomas Jefferson, September 25, 1803:

Whether the malignant fever, to which the large towns situated on the navigable waters of the United States are frequently subjected, are of local origin or imported is not, as it relates to this city, a fact of so much importance as that generally conceded of its propogation and virulence, depending on the state of the atmosphere. That it is invariably and most alarming and destructive in those situations which become the receptacle of the filth of the city, whether brought by the rain along the streets, or discharged through the common sewers. It is in the vicinity of the water, where the docks, slips, and other artificial obstruction to the regular and free current or stream of the river, retain the accumulated filth between the wharves that the air is vitiated. The mud and faeces are there exposed to the putrifying heat of the mid-day sun, for even at high water there is no current to carry it off into the stream. . . . The dreadful consequences are now suffered, when a radical cure will be attended with enormous expense. Happy may it be for the future inhabitants of the city of Washington if it profit by the experience of others, and before it is too late, adopt a system of improving the waters property, which . . . shall effectually remove the impurities brought into the river.

Official Report of Major General Robert Ross, British Commander, August 1814:

> Judging it of consequence to complete the destruction of the public buildings with the least possible delay, so that the army might retire without loss of time, the following buildings were set fire to and consumed: the Capitol, including the Senate-House and the House of Representatives, the arsenal, the dock-yard, (navy-yard), treasury, war office, President's palace, rope-walk, and the great bridge across the Potomac. . . . The object of the expedition being accomplished, I determined, before any greater force of the enemy could be assembled, to withdraw the troops, and accordingly commenced retiring on the night of the 25th.

Another British chronicler, Charles Ingersoll:

> The army which we had overthrown the day before, though defeated, was far from annihilated; and having by this time recovered its panic, began to concentrate itself on our front, and presented quite as formidable an appearance as ever. . . .
> Whether or not it was their intention to attack, I cannot pretend to say, because . . . soon after, when something like a movement could be discerned in their ranks, the sky grew suddenly dark, and the most tremendous hurricane . . . came on. Of the prodigious force of the wind, it is impossible for you to form any conception. Roofs of houses were torn off by it, and whisked into the air like sheets of paper; while the rain which accompanied it, resembled the rushing of a mighty cataract, rather than the dropping of a shower. The darkness was as great as if the sun had long set, and the last remains of twilight had come on, occasionally relieved by flashes of vivid lightning streaming through it, which, together with the noise of the wind and the thunder, the crash of falling buildings, and the tearing of roofs as they were stript from the walls, produced the most appalling effect. . . . This lasted for nearly two hours without intermission; during which time, many of the houses spared by us, were blown down, and thirty of our men, besides

several of the inhabitants, buried beneath their ruins. Our column was as completely dispersed, as if it had received a total defeat. . . .

By the time we reached the ground where yesterday's battles had been fought, the moon rose, and exhibited a spectacle by no means enlivening. The dead were still unburied, and lay about less in every direction, completely naked. They had been stripped even of their shirts; and, having been exposed in this state to the violent rain in the morning, they appeared to be bleached to a most unnatural degree of whiteness. The heat and rain together had likewise affected them in a different manner, and the smell which arose upon the night air was horrible.

---

1860:

Drinking water continued to be taken from wells and springs. There were but two little sewers, whose contents most annoyingly backed up into the cellars and shops of Pennsylvania Avenue. Along the northern edge of the rubbish-strewn Mall ran an open ditch, an enlargement of Tiber Creek—"floating," says an eyewitness, "dead cats and all kinds of putridity and reeking with pestilential odors."

---

Teddy Roosevelt described his joy, when he was president, in going out on rough cross-country walks, "perhaps down Rock Creek, which was then as wild as a stream in the White Mountains."

⟨interdigitation⟩

*Obedient to geology and climate are the varying plant and animal life of the Potomac, with a major boundary or, more properly, a zone of interdigitation, found in the area of Great Falls and the District of Columbia. In the heart of this area is Plummer's Island, known to the Indians as Winnemana, or Beautiful Island, where Upland flora and fauna have been found to mingle with those of Tidewater, and several new species have been discovered.*

# Transportation

1748, Thomas Cresap journeyed from his outpost settlement at Old
Town, to Williamsburg: floating with the current in the upper river,
avoiding rocks and shoals . . . portaging at Great Falls . . . then,
spreading sail for the easy cruise in the estuary and bay.

> Many of the prominent men of the colony were at the time in
> the Assembly in session at Williamsburg. The intelligent Cresap
> had no difficulty in interesting them in his view of the political
> and economic situation over the mountains. . . . A strong
> company was at once formed (1748) for trading with the Indians
> and establishing settlements in the western country. This was
> the organization of the Ohio Company.
>
> *Petition of John Hanbury to the King*
> *on behalf of the Ohio Company, 1748*
>
> . . . . . . . . . . . . . . . . . . . . . . . . . . . . . . . . . . . . . . . . . . . . . . . . . . . . . . . . . . .
>
> THAT Your Petitioners beg leave humbly to inform Your
> Majesty that the Lands to the West of the said Mountains are
> extremely fertile the Climate very fine and healthy and the Water
> of Mississippi and those of Potomac are only separated by One
> small Ridge of Mountains easily passable by Land Carriage from
> thence to the West of the Mountains and to the Branch of the
> Ohio and the Lake Erie British Goods may be carried at little
> Expence and afforded reasonably to the Indians in those Parts.

The Ohio Company—John Hanbury, George Mason, three Wash-
ingtons, and others—pursued the fur trade to the West.

Beginning at Alexandria—then called Belhaven—goods were
carried overland in wagons to the phantom town of Philae, above
the Great Falls; thence by water to the mouth of Wills Creek, where

a storehouse and fort were built. The fort came to be known as Fort Cumberland.

1752, Cresap was given the task of building a road from Wills Creek to the Monongahela. With an Indian, Nemacolin, he followed the path discovered a year earlier by Christopher Gist: over Wills, Savage and Meadow Mountains, into Little Meadows, over Briery Mountain and into the Great Meadows, thence over Laurel Hill via Red Stone Creek, to the Monongahela. The road was laid out and marked.

---

March 1755, the greatest armada ever seen on the river—a British fleet bearing 1,300 soldiers under command of General Braddock— entered the estuary of the Potomac.

> *Extracts from*
> A Journal of the Proceedings of the Detachment of Seamen, ordered by Commodore Kepple, to Afsist on the late Expedition to the *Ohio*. . . .
> April 10th Orders were given to March to Morrow with 6 Companies of S[r] P. Halket's Regiment for *Winchester* towards *Will's Creeks;* April 11th Yesterdays Orders were Countermanded and others given to furnish Eight days Provisions, to proceed to *Rock's Creek* (8 Miles from Alexandria) in the Sea Horse & Nightingale Boats; April 12th: Arrived at *Rock's Creek* 5 miles from the lower falls of *Potomack* & 4 Miles from the Eastern branch of it; where we encamped with Colonel Dunbars Regiment.
> April 13th: Employed in loading Waggon's with Stores Provisions and all other conveniences very near *Rock's Creek* a very pleasand Situation.
> April 14th: Detachment of Seamen were order'd to March in the Front: arrived at M[r] Lawrence Owen's: 15 Miles from *Rock's Creek;* and encamp'd upon good Ground 8 Miles from the Upper falls of *Potomack*
> April 15th: Encamp't on the side of a Hill near M[r] Michael Dowden's; 15 Miles from M[r] Owen's, in very bad Ground and in $1\frac{1}{2}$ foot Snow.

April 16th: Halted, but found it extremely difficult to get either Provisions or Forrage.

April 17th: March'd to *Fredericks Town;* 15 Miles from Dowden's, the road very Mountainous, March'd 11 Miles, when we came to a River call'd *Monskiso,* which emptied itself into the *Potomack;* it runs very rapid; and is, after hard Rain, 13 feet deep: We ferried over in a Float for that purpose. This Town has not been settled Above 7. Years; there are 200 Houses & 2 Churches 1 Dutch, 1 English; the inhabitants chiefly Dutch, Industrious, but imposing People; Provisions & Forrage in Plenty.

April 18th: Encamp'd with a New York Company under the Command of Captain Gates, at the North End of the Town, upon very good Ground

April 19th: Exercising Recruits, & airing the Tents: several Waggons arrived with Ordnance Stores, heavy Dews at Night occasion it to be very unwholsome.

April 20th: Nothing Material happen'd

April 21st: The General attended by Captains Orme, Morris and Secretary Shirley; with S[r] John S[t] Clair; arrived at Head Quarters.

April 24th

April 25th: Ordnance Stores Arrived, with 80 Recruits for the 2 Regiments

April 27th: Employ'd in preparing Harnefs for the Horses

April 29th: March'd to M[r] Walker's 18 Miles from Fredericks Town; pafs'd the South Ridge, commonly called the Blue Ridge, or *Shanandoh Mountains* Very easy Ascent and a fine Prospect. . no kind of Refreshment

April 30th: March'd to *Connecochiag;* 16 Miles from M[r] Walker's Close by the *Potomack,* a very fine Situation, where we found all the Artillery Stores preparing to go by Water to Wills Creek

May 1st: Employed in ferrying (over the *Potomack*) the Army Baggage into Virginia in 2 Floats and 5 Batteaux; The Army March'd to M[r] John Evans, 16 Miles from y[e] *Potomack* and 20 Miles from Winchester, where we Encamp'd, and had tolerable good living with Forrage; the roads begin to be very indifferent

May 2nd: Halted and sent the Horses to Grafs

May 3ʳᵈ: March'd to Widdow Barringers 18 Miles from Mͬ Evans; the day was so excessive hot, that many Officers and Men could not Arrive at their Ground until Evening, this is 5 Miles from Winchester and a fine Situation

May 4ᵗʰ: March'd to Mͬ Pots 9 Miles from the Widdow's where we were refresh' with Vinison and wild Turkeys the Roads excefsive bad.

May 5ᵗʰ: March'd to Mͬ Henry Enocks, a place called the *forks of Cape Capon,* 16 Miles from Mͬ Pots; over prodigious Mountains, and between the Same we crofs'd a Run of Water in 3 Miles distance, 20 times after marching 15 Miles we came to a River called *Kahepatin* where the Army ferried over, We found a Company of Sͬ Peter Halkets Regiment waiting to escort the Train of Artillery to *Wills Creek*

May 6ᵗʰ: Halted, as was the Custom to do every third day, The Officers for pafsing away the time, made Horse Races and agreed that no Horse should Run over 11 Hands and to carry 14 Stone

May 7ᵗʰ: March'd to Mͬ Cox's by the side of yᵉ *Potomack* 12 miles from Mͬ Enock's, and Encamped we crofs'd another run of Water 19 Times in 2 Miles. Roads bad.

May 8ᵗʰ: Ferried over the River into *Maryland;* and March'd to Mͬ Jacksons, 8 Miles from Mͬ Cox's where we found a Maryland Company encamp'd in a fine Situation on the Banks of the *Potomack;* with clear'd ground about it; there lives Colonel Crefsop, a Rattle Snake Colonel, and a D-d Rascal; calls himself a Frontiersman, being nearest the *Ohio*; he had a Summons some time since from the French to retire from his Settlement, which they claim'd as their property, but he refused it like a man of Spirit; This place is the Track of Indian Warriours, when going to War, either to the Nºward, or Sºward He hath built a little Fort round his House, and is resolved to keep his Ground. We got plenty of Provisions &c. The General arrived with Captains Orme and Morris, with Secretary Shirley and a Company of light Horse for his Guard, under the command of Capͭ Stewart, the General lay at the Colonels.

May 9ᵗʰ: Halted and made another Race to amuse the General

D⁰. 10ᵗʰ: March'd to *Will's Creek;* and Encamp'd on a Hill to the Eᵗward of the Fort, when the General past the Troops; Colonel Dunbar informed them, that there were a number of Indians at *Wills Creek,* that were Friends to English therefore it was the Generals positive Orders, that they should not be Molested upon any account, upon the Generals Arrival at the Fort, He was Saluted with 17. Guns, and we found 100 Indian Men, Women & Children with 6 Companies of Sʳ Peter Halketts Regiment, 9 Virginian Companies and a Maryland Company.

May 11ᵗʰ: *Fort Cumberland,* is situated within 200 Yards of *Wills Creek* on a Hill 400 Yards from the *Potomack,* it's greatest length from East to West is 200 Yards, and breadth 40 it is built with Loggs drove into the Ground; and 12 feet above it Embrazures are cut for 12 Guns which are 4. Pounders, though 10 are only Mounted with Loopholes for small Arms; The Indians were greatly surprised at the regular way of our Soldiers Marching and our Numbers.

General Braddock, Fort Cumberland, June 5, 1755:

On the 10th of May I arriv'd at this place, and on the 17th the train join'd me from Alexandria after a March of twenty seven days, having met with many more Delays and Difficulties than I had even apprehended, from the Badness of the Roads, Scarcity of Forage, and a general Want of Spirit in the people to forward the Expedition.

I have at last collected the whole Force with which I propose to march to the Attack of Fort Duquesne, amounting to about two thousand effective Men, eleven hundred of which Number are Americans of the southern provinces, whose slothful and languid Disposition renders them very unfit for Military Service. I have employ'd the properest officers to form and discipline them and great pains has and shall be taken to make them as useful as possible. . . .

It would be endless, Sir, to particularize the numberless Instances of the Want of public and private Faith, and of the most absolute Disregard of all Truth, which I have met with in carrying on of His Majesty's Service on this continent.

The Journal again: "June 10th: the last Division of His Majesty's Forces March'd from *Wills Creek* with General Braddock."

Cutting the road as they went, through a "wooden country," the army stretched out to a length of four miles: over Will's Mountain, up Braddock's Run to the forks, into the valley of George's Creek, over Savage Mountain, through dense white pine forests, near the tract known as *Shades of Death,* to the Little Meadows . . . marching in regular formation, to the Monongahela.

---

      Buffalo trace,
            Indian trail,
                       Nemacolin's path. . .
      Braddock's Road,
              The National Road. . .

An act of Congress, April 30, 1802, enabled the people of Ohio to form a state government.

That one-twentieth of the net proceeds of the lands lying within said State sold by Congress shall be applied to the laying out and making public roads leading from the navigable waters emptying into the Atlantic, to the Ohio, to the the said state, and through the same, such roads to be laid out under the authority of Congress with the consent of the several states through which the roads shall pass.

AN ACT TO REGULATE THE LAYING OUT AND MAKING A ROAD FROM CUMBERLAND, IN THE STATE OF MARYLAND, TO THE STATE OF OHIO
      SECTION 1. *Be it enacted by the Senate and House of Representatives of the United States of America in Congress assembled,* That the President of the United States be, and he is hereby authorized to appoint, by and with the advice and consent of the Senate, three discreet and disinterested citizens of the United States, to lay out a road from Cumberland . . . in the state of Maryland . . . to the state of Ohio; whose duty it shall be . . . to repair to

Cumberland aforesaid, and view the ground, from the points on the river Potomac . . . to the river Ohio; and to lay out in such direction as they shall judge, under all circumstances the most proper, a road from thence to the river Ohio. . . .

SEC. 2 And be it further enacted, That the aforesaid road shall be laid out four rods in width, and designated on each side by a plain and distinguishable mark on a tree, or by the erection of a stake or monument sufficiently conspicuous, in every quarter of a mile of the distance at least. . . .

SEC. 3 And be it further enacted, That the commissioners shall as soon as may be, after they have laid out the road, as aforesaid, present to the President an accurate plan of the same, with its several courses and distances, accompanied by a written report. . . .

SEC. 4 And be it further enacted, That all parts of the road which the President shall direct to be made, in case the trees are standing, shall be cleared the whole width of four rods; and the road shall be raised in the middle of the carriage-way with stone, earth, or gravel or sand. . . .

SEC. 5 And be it further enacted, That said commissioners shall receive four dollars per day, while employed as aforesaid, in full compensation. . . .

SEC. 6 And be it further enacted, That the sum of thirty thousand dollars be, and the same is hereby appropriated, to defray the expenses of laying out and making said road. . . .

Approved March 29, 1806.

TH. JEFFERSON.

The commissioners, December 30, 1806,

beg leave to report to the President of the United states, and to premise that the duties imposed by the law became a work of greater magnitude, and a task much more arduous, than was conceived before entering upon it. . . .

The face of the country within the limits prescribed is generally very uneven, and in many places broken by a succession of high mountains and deep hollows, too formidable to be reduced within five degrees of the horizon, but by crossing them obliquely, a mode which, although it imposes a heavy task of hill-side digging, obviates generally the necessity of reducing hills and filling hollows, which, on these grounds, would be an attempt truly quixotic.

———————

The road was finally built, Cumberland to Wheeling, at an average cost of $13,000 per mile.

Wagoners and stage drivers, regulars and sharpshooters, Indians, pony express and mail robbers, all navigated the pike . . . Henry Puffenberger and Jacob Breakiron were wagoners, David Bone-breaker drove a stage, Dumb Ike and Crazy Billy were pike characters.

Taverns were built: the Black Tavern, Thistle Tavern, Temple of Juno, selling "strong waters to relieve the inhabitants," and stogies, four for a penny. Teamsters ate, drank, smoked, danced, bragged and fought . . . slept on the floor, feet to fireplace.

A wagoner recalled,

> I have stayed over night with William Sheets, on Nigger Mountain, when there would be thirty six-horse teams on the wagon yard, one hundred Kentucky mules in an adjacent lot, one thousand hogs in other enclosures, and as many fat cattle from Illinois in adjoining fields. The music made by this large number of hogs, in eating corn on a frosty night, I will never forget.

———————

Geo. Washington, May 4, 1772:

> An Act has passed this session empowering Trustees (to be chosen by ye Subscribers to the Scheme) to raise money by way of Subscription, & Lottery, for the purpose of opening, and extending the Navigation of Potomack from the Tide Water, to Fort Cumberland.

*1784*

*September*

Having found it indispensably necessary to visit my Landed property West of the Apalachean Mountains . . . and having made the necessary preparations for it, I did, on the first day of this Month (September) set out on my journey.

3d. Colo. Warner Washington, Mr. Wormeley, Gen'l Morgan, Mr. Trickett, and many other Gentlemen came here to see me— and one object of my journey being to obtain information of the nearest and best communication between the Eastern and Western Waters; and to facilitate as much as in me lay the inland Navigation of the Potomac; I conversed a good deal with Gen'l Morgan on this subject. . . .

10th . . . After leaving the Waters of Wills Creek which extends up the Mountain (Alligany) two or three Miles as the Road goes, we fell next on those of George's Creek, which are small— after them, upon Savage River which are considerable: tho' from the present appearance of them, does not seem capable of Navigation.

26th . . . I could obtain no good acct. of the Navigation of the No. Branch between McCulloch's crossing and Will's Creek (or Fort Cumberland) indeed there were scarce any persons of whom enqueries could be made . . . but in general I could gather . . . that there is no fall in it—that from Fort Cumberland to the Mouth of Savage River the water being good is frequently made use of in its present State with Canoes—and from thence upwards, is only rapid in places with loose Rocks which can readily be removed.

*October*

4th The more then the Navigation of Potomack is investigated, duly considered, the greater the advantages . . . appear.

. . . These two alone (that is the South Branch and Shannon-doah) would afford water transportation for all that fertile Country between the Bleu Ridge and the Alligany Mountains; which is immense. . . .

Let us open a good communication with the Settlements west of us—extend the inland Navigation as far as it can be done with convenience—and shew them by this means, how easy it is to bring the produce of their Lands to our Markets, and see how astonishingly our exports will be increased. . . .

Having gone so far, I will hazard another idea in proof of my opinion of this navigation. . . . It is, that the Navigation from the Great Falls and through the Shenandoah falls, will not be opened *five* years before that of the latter River will be improved *at least* 150 miles; and the whole produce of that rich and extensive vale between the Blue ridge and the Alligany Mountains be brought through *it,* and the *South Branch,* as far South Westerly as Staunton into the Potomack; and thence by the Great falls to the place or places of Exportation. Add this to what will be drawn from the upper part of Maryland, and parts of Pensylvania (which at present go to Baltimore by an expensive land transportation) and then annex thereto the idea of what may come (under a wise policy) from the Western waters, and it opens a field almost too extensive for imagination. . . .

Let the benefits arising from water transportation, be once felt . . . everything within its vortex . . . will be sucked into, and be transported by water.

Washington to the Marquis de Lafayette:

As the clouds which overspread your hemisphere are dispersing, and peace with all its concomitants is drawing upon your Land, I will banish the sound of War from my letter: I wish to see the sons and daughters of the world in Peace and busily employed in the more agreable amusement of fulfilling the first and great commandment, *Increase and Multiply:* as an encouragement to which we have opened the fertile plains of the Ohio to the poor, the needy and the oppressed of the Earth; any one therefore who is heavy laden, or who wants land to cultivate, may repair thither and abound, as in the Land of promise, with milk and honey: the ways are preparing, and the roads will be made easy thro' the channels of Potomac.

From a notice in the *Virginia Gazette,* December 4, 1784:

> At a numerous and respectable meeting held the 12th. of last month at Alexandria by gentlemen of this state and Maryland to deliberate and consult on the vast great political and commercial object, the rendering navigable the Potomack River from tide water, it was unanimously resolved that every possible effort ought to be exerted to render those waters navigable to their utmost sources. . . . This is perhaps a work of more political than commercial consequence as it will be one of the grandest chains for preserving Federal Union. The western world will have free access to us and we shall be one and the same people.

May 17th, 1785, in Alexandria, the Patowmack Company was formally organized, with George Washington president. Original plans called for opening the river from Tidewater to Fort Cumberland, so that a minimum of fifty barrels of flour could move downstream in even the driest season. Boulders in the stream bed were to be blasted at Seneca and Shenandoah Falls, and a canal built at Great Falls. Washington felt that locks would not be needed, even at Great Falls:

> The Water through these Falls is of sufficient depth for good navigation; and as formidable as I had conceived them to be; but by no means impractible. The principal difficulties lye in rocks which occasion a crooked passage. These once removed, renders the passage safe without the aid of Locks.

Later, it was found necessary to build canals at five falls—House's, Shenandoah, Seneca, Little, and Great—with locks at the latter two.

Washington looked for a man to superintend operations: a man "who knows best how to conduct water upon a level, or who can carry it thro' hills or over Mountains, that would be most useful to us."

The name of James Rumsey came to his attention:

As I have imbibed a very favorable opinion of your mechanical abilities, and have had no reason to distrust your fitness in other respects; I took the liberty of mentioning your name to the Directors, and I dare say if you are disposed to offer your services, they would be attended to under favorable circumstances.

James Rumsey: inventor, before Fulton, of the steamboat. 1784, armed with a testimonial from Washington, he secured from the Virginia legislature an exclusive right to build and navigate boats on Virginia waters, for the next ten years. December 1787, at Steamboat Bend on the Potomac, above Shepherdstown, he fired up the boiler and his first steamer chugged upstream, attaining speeds of three miles an hour. A week later, the pipes froze and burst, but he stuffed them with rags, and got her up to four miles an hour.

Meanwhile, he agreed to take over management of the Patowmack Company.

Washington:

We expect to begin our operations on the Patowmack Navigation about the 6th of next Month, under the Management of a Mr. James Rumsey. If the Miners therefore, who have been accustomed to the blowing of Rocks under Water, are desirous of employment in this way, I am persuaded he would hire them, were they to apply to him, either at the Seneca falls, or the Falls of Shannondoah.

To Geo. Wm. Fairfax:

We have commenced our operations on the navigation of this river; and I am happy to inform you, that the difficulties rather vanish than increase as we proceed.

Three classes of labor were secured: hired whites, indentured whites, and Negro slaves—none of whom got along with one another.

Washington:

> We are endeavoring to engage our miners to bore by the foot;
> rather than by the day; but as yet have not agreed with any in
> this way; they ask a shilling, which we think is too much to
> common labourers we pay 40/ per month; and we find paying
> the workmen every fortnight rather troublesome once a month
> would do better: as they will be frequently moving, we have
> provided Tents as most convenient and least expensive, for their
> accommodation.

For daily rations, laborers received one pound salt pork, or one and a
quarter pounds salt beef, or one and a half pounds fresh beef or
mutton, one and a half pounds flour or bread, three gills of rum.

The Irish day laborers tended to run away. As for the others—from
the *Maryland Chronicle*, February 22, 1786:

> We hear that several servants who had been purchased to work
> on the Potowmack Navigation lately ran away, but being soon
> after apprehended, were sentenced to have their heads & eye-
> brows shaved, which operation was immediately executed.

Rumsey reported to Mr. Hartshorne, company treasurer:

> Great Falls potowmack July 3d 1786. Sir We have Been much
> Imposed upon the last Two weeks in the powder way (we had
> two Blowers, One Run off the other Blown up) we therefore
> was Obliged to have two new hands put to Blowing and there
> was much attention gave to them least Axedents should happen
> yet they used the powder Rather too Extravagent, But that was
> not all they have certainly stolen a Considerable Quantity as we
> have not more by us than will last until tomorrow noon. Our
> hole troop is Such Villians.

At Little Falls, the lock pits were dug, and hasty and impermanent
wooden locks erected. At Great Falls, Washington insisted that the
canal be cut on the Virginia side.

After an early breakfast at Mr. Fairfax's Gov'r. Johnson and I set out for the Falls (accompanied by Mr. Fairfax) where we met the other Directors and Colo. Gilpin in the operation of levelling the ground for the proposed cut or Canal from the place where it is proposed to take the Water out, to the other where it will be let into the River again. In the highest of which, and for near 70 Rod, it is between five or seven feet higher than the Surface of the Water at the head. After which it descends, and for at least 300 yards at the lower end, rapidly. This cut, upon the whole, does not appear to be attended with more difficulty than was apprehended.

But the cut proved to be through solid rock . . .

> At the Great falls the labour has indeed been great; the water there is taken into a canal about 200 yards above the Cataract and conveyed by a level cut (thro' a solid rock in some places and very stoney ground in others) more than a mile to the lock seats; five in number, by means of which the Craft when these locks are compleated will be let into the River below the fall (which in all is 76 feet).

Five locks were eventually constructed at Great Falls—

> Blown out of the solid rock, the natural rock worked tolerably smooth forming the sides, some mason work being used where the fixtures are inserted for supporting the gates, the sluice gates in these locks as in several of the others that are deep, do not lift but are made of cast iron and turn on a pivot fixed in the center, so that when the sluice is open this little gate or stopper is turned edgewise to the stream, they work very easy and are managed in deep locks much more readily than those of the ordinary construction.

Some of the hewn blocks, of Triassic sandstone, were ferried across the river from Seneca, and into each block the stonecutter carved his trademark: roman numerals, or an indecipherable glyph.

From the president's report, 1801:

> It must appear evident that without some unforeseen accident
> the great object held out in our last report, that of a free naviga-
> tion of the Potomac during a considerable portion of the year
> from the mouth of George's Creek to tide water will be accom-
> plished by the end of the year in time for the ensuing spring
> water.

The trustees laid out a town at Great Falls to be called Matildaville,
with forge, sawmill, grist mill, superintendent's house, etc. (laid
out, but never built).

In February 1802, the locks were opened for business.

Attention turned now to improving the riverbed upstream, and on
the Shenandoah:

Washington:

> At the foot of these falls the Directors and myself (Govr. Lee
> having joined us the Evening before) held a meeting. At which
> it was determined, as we conceived the Navigation could be
> made through these (commonly called the Shannondoah) Falls
> without the aid of Locks, and by opening them would give eclat
> to the undertaking and great ease to the upper Inhabitants. . . .
>    The Shannondoah will intercept every article 200 miles from
> its mouth, and water bear it to the Markets.

Channels in the Potomac were to be improved by banking with
saplings and brush loaded with stone.

With locks and channels open, farmers moved their crops to market.
Water craft were mostly floats or rafts, designed according to the
harvest and the size of the locks. On delivery of the cargo at Georgetown, they were broken up and sold for firewood. A few permanent
boats were built, seventy feet by ten feet, covered with tarpaulins

over hoops, and manned by crews of four. Two gallons of whiskey, four tin cups, thirty pounds of bacon, and twenty feet of rope were standard supplies for a trip from Cumberland to Georgetown. After unloading, the boats were roped and poled back upstream, against the current.

Principal downstream cargoes were flour, whiskey, iron, and tobacco, and trade goods went out from Georgetown, via the Potomac, to points on Lake Erie, the Missouri River and the Gulf of Mexico.

Difficulties for the Potomac Company, however, were endless. Subscribers failed to pay up, revenues were low and loans difficult to secure, the river channels were inconstant, temporary wooden locks had to be replaced with stone and masonry—and there was always either too much or too little water: at times the forty-foot rock at Great Falls was covered, in flood—while at others a flat-boat could scarcely be floated in the channel approaching it.

In 1799, Washington died.

From the report of a Virginia state commission, July 1822:

> . . . that the affairs of the Potomac Company have failed to comply with the terms and conditions of the charter; that there was no reasonable ground to expect that they would be able to effect the objects of their incorporation; that they have not only expended their capital stock and the tolls received, with the exception of a small dividend of five dollars and fifty cents on each share declared in 1802, but had incurred a heavy debt which their resources would never enable them to discharge; that the floods and freshets nevertheless gave the only navigation that was enjoyed; that the whole time when produce and goods could be stream bourne on the Potomac in the course of an entire year, did not exceed forty-five days; that it would be imprudent and inexpedient to give further aid to the Potomac Company.

A report by Thomas Moore, Virginia engineer, August 1820:

> But when the powers of art have been exerted to the utmost
> extent to procure an easy navigation in the bed of a stream, still
> it must hold a very inferior grade to that of an independent
> canal, because the natural fall of the river must be overcome by
> the labor of men, and . . . in proportion to the length must be
> very expensive compared with a canal furnished with locks,
> where the loaded boats are drawn on level water, by the labor of
> horses.

Virginia Board of Public Works, to the legislature, 1823:

> The estimates of the probable cost necessary for constructing an
> independent canal along the valley of the Potomac river from
> Cumberland to tide water—185 miles. . . .
>     Total with contingencies    $2,000,000

Resolution passed by a convention meeting in Washington, November 6, 1823:

> Whereas, a connection of the Atlantic and Western waters, by a
> canal, leading from the seat of the general government to the
> river Ohio, regarded as a local object, is one of the highest im-
> portance to the states immediately interested therein, and, con-
> sidered in a national view, is of inestimable consequence to the
> future union, security, and happiness of the United States:
>     *Resolved, unanimously,* That it is expedient to substitute, for
> the present defective navigation of the Potomac river above tide
> water, a navigable canal, by Cumberland to the mouth of Sav-
> age Creek, at the eastern base of the Alleghany and to extend
> such canal.

Although constructed, finally, only to Cumberland, the canal was
surveyed through to Pittsburgh, via Wills Creek, Casselman's River,
and the Youghiogheny.

1828, the remaining property of the Potomac Company was conveyed to the Chesapeake and Ohio Canal Company.

That summer, President John Quincy Adams took part in groundbreaking ceremonies for the canal: "To subdue the earth is preeminently the purpose of the undertaking."

> On the same day—July 4—work was started on the Baltimore and Ohio Railroad . . .

Workmen were hard to find, particularly skilled stonemasons, for construction of the locks. The company advertised in Dublin, Cork, and Belfast, offering "meat three times a day, a reasonable amount of liquor and $8, $10, $12 a week." Beginning in 1829, the Irish laborers poured in, went to work with trowel, ax, chisel, and hammer; horse, cart, scraper; wheelbarrow, drill, and gunpowder . . .

Every summer, the sickly season arrived, the workers associated their aches and fevers with the low waters, the murky, malodorous riverbed.

August 1832, Asiatic cholera appeared, and was soon general from Harper's Ferry, down to Point of Rocks.

> If the Board but imagine the panic produced by a man's turning black and dying in twenty four hours in the very room where his comrades are to sleep or to dine they will readily conceive the utility of separating the sick, dying and dead from the living.

> Before this letter reaches Washington, the whole line of canal from the point of rocks to WmsPort will be abandoned by the Contractors and Laborers—The Cholera has appeared amongst them, and has proved fatal in almost every case. There has been upwards of 30 deaths nearly opposite to us since friday last, and the poor Exiles of Erin are flying in every direction. . . . It is candidly my opinion, that by the last of this week you will not have a working man on the whole line.

They have since been suffering great mortality west of Harper's Ferry, & I fear the work is by this time suspended. The poor creatures, after seeing a few sudden & awful deaths amongst their friends, straggled off in all directions through the country; but for very many of them the panic came too late. They are dying in all parts of Washington County at the distance of 5 to 15 miles from the river. I myself saw numbers of them in carts & on foot making their way towards Pennsylvania.

Following the cholera came warfare between rival factions:

January 1834, there was a preliminary skirmish between Corkonians from above Williamsport, and the Longfords, or Fardowners, from below the town. Several were killed before militia arrived. Local citizens patrolled the Conococheague aqueduct, while both sides collected weapons, and the countryside took on the appearance of an armed camp. January 24, the Longfords marched in force, 300 strong, armed with guns, clubs, and helves. Crossing the aqueduct, they met 300 Corkonians on a hilltop, near Dam No. 5, and there was a pitched battle, with several casualties. Two companies of U.S. troops finally arrived from Fort McHenry . . .

New Year's Day, 1838, a number of Irish raided their rivals at Oldtown, and Nicholas Ryan's tavern was nearly demolished. The men were pursued by a sheriff's posse, but all escaped . . .

When finally completed in 1850, the Chesapeake and Ohio Canal was 184½ miles long, from Rock Creek in the District of Columbia to Wills Creek at Cumberland, Maryland. There were seven rubble or masonry dams in the bed of the river, eleven stone aqueducts over the northern tributaries, seventy-five stone or composition locks with a lift averaging eight feet, many score culverts to carry the smaller streams under the trunk, a quarter-mile long tunnel, and a towpath twelve feet wide, on the river side of the canal. The waterway itself was six to eight feet deep, and fifty to eighty feet wide. Total descent was 578 feet.

Final cost—estimated originally at $2,000,000—came to over $11,000,000.

Service was imperfect, especially during the early years: employees and boatmen were green; construction sometimes proved shoddy; there was too much water—or too little water; and there were leaks—with or without the help of muskrats. Obstructions included fallen rocks, sunken wrecks, loose boats, dead animals . . .

Banks of the canal were built to withstand the worst possible floods, that of 1847 having been the highest in sixty years. But in 1852, the water rose six feet higher, reaching sixty-four feet at Great Falls. Damage was extensive.

1857, a great ice freshet, followed by successive spring floods, flowed down the valley, ripping holes in the dams.

1861–64, Confederates under Lee, Early, Mosby, and White burned boats, stole mules, and sabotaged banks, dams, and locks.

November 1877, came the worst flood in 150 years, the water at Great Falls rose to seventy feet above low-water. Walls, towpath, and even the masonry dams were breached, tools, stores, and cargoes were lost.

> All the floods were the result of rapid deforestation and deep plowing in the Potomac watershed . . .

May 30, 1889, a "cyclone" entered the valley near Martinsburg, crossed the river above Williamsport, and was followed by torrential rains. The river rose, kept on rising, to points in excess of the flood of '77. The junction of Potomac and Conococheague became a lake. At Sandy Hook, opposite Harper's Ferry, water reached a point eight feet higher than the railroad tracks, which were, in turn, seventeen feet above the canal. Frame buildings, roped to trees, broke loose; cargoes, boats, and drowned teams were strewn crazily down the valley. . . .

One of the peculiarities of the freshet of 1889 is that the stone-work of the walls, &c., is more generally involved than on any previous occasion of the kind. The telephone wires have been swept away . . . and every bridge for which the canal company is responsible is down.

Damage was estimated at close to a million dollars. The canal was repaired . . .

         . . . but the flood of '89 marked the beginning of the end.

---

*Regulations*
*For Navigating the*
*Chesapeake and Ohio Canal.*

1st. Every Boat or Float, navigating the Canal after the 15th day of August next, shall be propelled by a towing line drawn by men or horses, and shall be moreover furnished with strapping or snubbing lines for passing through the locks of the Canal without injury to the same.

3d. No Boat or Float shall forcibly strike, or violently rub against any other boat, or against the banks, locks, aquaducts, inside walls, or wastes, or bridges of the Canal.

8th. No Carcafs, or dead animal, or putrid substance of any kind, shall be thrown into the Canal, or into any basin or feeder connected therewith.

11th. No raft or tow of timber pafsing on the Canal, shall consist of more than eight cribs, and when consisting of more than one, they shall be so united, as to conform readily to the curvatures of the Canal banks, and to glide by the same without rubbing against them.

15th. . . . As soon as she has opened a pafsage for the other, so as that the tow-line may sink to the bottom of the Canal, the boat entitled to pafs shall float over the tow-line.

16th. No Boat or Float, unlefs specially licensed to travel with greater speed, shall move on the Canal . . . with a velocity exceeding four miles an hour.

Boats carrying U.S. mail had the right-of-way over passenger packets, the latter over freight, and all boats over rafts. Boats descending prevailed over boats ascending. Right-of-way was yielded by turning to the berm side, away from the towpath, and slowing to a halt.

Most of the boats came from boatyards along the basin at the head of the canal. They were built of oak and white pine, fine two- and three-inch planks, sixty and seventy-five feet long, cut in the Cumberland hills. Generally, they were ninety-seven by fourteen feet, with five-foot draught, dimensions fixed by the size of the lock chambers. The flat bottoms, curved at bow and stern, were tarred; above the water line the boats were painted white, with green trim. Capacity was 125 tons. There was a stable for the mules at the bow, a hayhouse amidships, and a cabin at the stern.

Steamboats were introduced, but they were costly, burning too much coal in proportion to cargo capacity. Mules, slower but cheaper, were finally used universally. They were broken by hitching them to logs. If a green mule tended to sit down, he was hitched to a couple of trained mules and dragged along, until he found it more comfortable to stand.

> At Point of Rocks, where the Catoctins edge into the river, the Canal and the Railroad had contested for years for a narrow strip of ledge, forty feet wide. The courts finally herded them both through, but required the railroad to build a solid fence, to shield the mules from the steam engines.

An average trip, Cumberland to Georgetown, loaded with coal, took five days. Coming back light, you could make it in three days, sixty to seventy miles a day.

The halfway stake was nailed to a big elm on the four-mile level above Big Slack Water. There was a haunted house on the lower nine-mile level . . .

A lock-keeper, on duty day and night, received his house, an acre for a garden, and $150 a year. Married men with large families were preferred: more hands to do the work. Many supplemented their income selling liquor to the boatmen.

. . . Unless the boatmen were shipping whiskey, in which case they could always tap one barrel for a gallon, and refill with water.

Boatmen were a special breed, living on their boats, wintering in settlements away from towns, marrying from among themselves, so that children grew up knowing no other life. . . . It was a family affair: Mrs. Wes Lizer was known up and down the water for her apple dumplings, while Scat Eaton's wife made the best pie, from blackberries picked along the towpath.

Piney Wine, Dent Shupp, Daze Wolf, Rufus Stride, Oth Grove, Rome Mose, John Keysucker and Charlie Shawt, all boated the canal.

And there was Johnny Howard, who got into a fight with his captain and killed him. He was hanged in the Cumberland jail yard, March 17, 1876. A song was written about him; Annie Stride "used to play it on the piano and sing it until people cried. It was so sad. Annie boated, too. She could steer better than Ben could."

Off hours in Cumberland, a boatman headed for Shantytown, for drinkin' and fightin', at Old Aunt Susan Jones's Rising Sun Saloon.

———————

In the Paw Paw Bends, the canal tunneled through the knobby spur of a 2,000-foot mountain. The tunnel was brick lined; wrought-iron posts with chestnut stringers edged the towpath. From a rocky ledge above the towpath, just outside the tunnel, the boats took on drinking water from the finest cold spring.

Negro hands refused to boat through the tunnel, clambering instead over the mountain: they believed the tunnel haunted by a headless man.

Once two boats entered the tunnel at the same time from opposite ends: meeting in the middle, both refused to yield, and they stayed there for days, blocking traffic—until finally the company built a fire in the middle and smoked them out.

---

1923: The water was let out of the ditch at the end of the boating season.

Many of the locktenders and locktenders' widows stayed on, beside locks ruined by flood and neglect . . . Tom Moore at Mountain Lock, Mrs. Lucy Zimmerman at No. 39, Lewis Cross at Catoctin, and Emma Fulton at Point of Rocks.

---

Washington's Birthday, 1939, the C & O Canal, comprising 5,250 acres, was dedicated as a public park. A 38-year-old mule named Mutt took part in the ceremonies. The canal was partly restored, but subsequently there were floods . . .

*Above:* Robert E. Lee photographed in his
house in Richmond by Brady. 1865.
*(The Library of Congress)*
*Opposite:* General Grant photographed by
Brady at his headquarters at City Point,
Virginia, before the battle of Spotsylvania.
*(The Library of Congress)*

*Above:* A temporary pontoon bridge on the James River. *(The Library of Congress)*
*Opposite Top:* A dead soldier photographed by Brady at Fredericksburg. 1863.
*(The Library of Congress)*
*Opposite Bottom:* Yorktown fortifications of the Union army. Photograph by Brady. 1862.
*(The Library of Congress)*

*Top:* Photograph of John Wilkes Booth as a young man. *(The Library of Congress)* *Bottom:* Execution of the Lincoln conspirators. Photograph by Brady. *(The Library of Congress)*

*Top:* The Great Falls of the Potomac, about
fifteen miles above Washington.
*(The Library of Congress)*
*Bottom:* Harpers Ferry at the meeting of the
Shenandoah and Potomac Rivers. 1865.
*(The National Archives)*

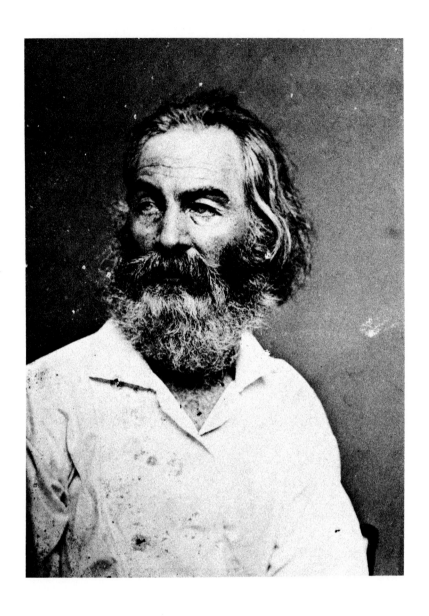

Photograph of Walt Whitman made by Brady
in the 1860s. *(The Library of Congress)*

*Average annual temperature for the entire Potomac basin is 54° Fahrenheit, with recorded extremes of 30° below zero and 112° above. Mean precipitation is 38 inches a year, and snowfall varies from 5 inches on the Coastal Plain to 30 inches on the Allegheny Plateau. The river is divided into two distinct areas of climate, with separate sources of storm systems. The Blue Ridge serves as a border: eastward, the major storms have been associated with the movement northward and northeastward of low pressure areas, including the West Indian hurricanes; whereas west of the Ridge major storms are generally of the frontal type, producing precipitation of long duration, low intensity, and even distribution.*

*With such variations in climate, both seasonally and erratically, the Potomac is subject to great variations in stream flow. During the flood of March 1936, an estimated 480,000 cubic feet per second flowed past Point of Rocks; on September 16, 1914, the recorded discharge fell to 540 cubic feet per second. Generally, the flow is heavy in spring, and low in late summer and early fall.*

*Roughly 12 percent of the population of the United States lives in the Potomac River basin. Of the land surface, 55 percent is forested, 23 percent is cropland, 16 percent pasture, 2 percent urban, and 4 percent miscellaneous. For the remainder of this century it is predicted that forest land will remain nearly stable, but that urban and suburban areas will gain heavily at the expense of crop and pasture lands.*

# Civil War

JOHN BROWN

May 8, 1858, Chatham, Ontario, the Provisional Constitutional Convention was held. There was a reading of the Provisional Constitution and Ordinance for the People of the United States:

> Whereas, slavery throughout its entire existence in the United States is none other than a most barbarous, unprovoked, and unjustifiable war of one portion of its citizens upon another portion. . . .

The following officers were elected:

> Secretary of War—John Henry Kagi
> Secretary of State—Richard Realf
> Secretary of the Treasury—George Gill
> Treasurer—Owen Brown
> Members of Congress—Osborn P. Anderson
>                          A. M. Ellsworth
> and,
> Commander-in-Chief: John Brown

Brown, October 21, 1859:

> I wish to say, furthermore, that you had better—all you people at the South—prepare yourselves for a settlement of that question that must come up for settlement sooner than you are prepared for it. . . . This question is still to be settled—this negro question I mean; the end of that is not yet.

------

July 1859, Brown, with twenty-two associates, rented the Kennedy farm, on the Maryland side, not far from Harper's Ferry. During the day, the men were confined to the loft, to avoid arousing suspicion of the neighbors. Housework was done mostly by Brown's two young daughters-in-law.

Osborn P. Anderson:

> As we could not circulate freely, they would bring in wild fruit and flowers from the woods and fields. We were well supplied with grapes, paw-paws, chestnuts, and other small fruit, besides bouquets of fall flowers, through their thoughtful consideration.
>
> During the several weeks I remained at the encampment, we were under the restraint I write of through the day; but at night, we sallied out for a ramble, or to breathe the fresh air and enjoy the beautiful solitude of the mountain scenery around, by moonlight.

John Brown, October 16:

> And now, gentlemen, let me impress this one thing upon your minds. You all know how dear life is to you, and how dear your life is to your friends. And in remembering that, consider that the lives of others are as dear to them as yours are to you. Do not, therefore, take the life of any one, if you can possibly avoid it; but if it is necessary to take life in order to save your own, then make sure work of it.

Kagi:

> This is just the right time. The year's crops have been good, and they are now perfectly housed, and in the best condition for use. The moon is just right. Slaves are discontented at this season.

October 16, 1859, after dark:

John Brown, commander-in-chief of the Provisional Army: "Men, get on your arms; we will proceed to the Ferry."

Horse and wagon were brought to the door, and pikes, fagots, a sledge-hammer, and a crowbar were loaded. The men buckled on their arms and threw over their shoulders long gray shawls, to conceal the arms. Captain Owen Brown and privates Coppoc and Meriam remained behind, in charge of arms and supplies, and to marshal the runaway slaves that were expected to join them. John Brown put on his battle-worn Kansas cap, mounted the wagon, and led his army of eighteen, marching in double column, down the little lane to the road, and on to Harper's Ferry.

The night was cloudy, damp and dark; the army met no one on the six-mile march.

Captains Cook and Tidd, their commissions signed, sealed, and in their pockets, went on ahead, to destroy telegraph wires on both Maryland and Virginia sides. Following them were Kagi and Stevens, as advance guard. Entering the Maryland bridge at 10:30 P.M., they took William Williams, the watchman, as their first prisoner. Williams thought it all a joke until the gun muzzles were in his face. Crossing the bridge, the men passed the Wager House—combined hotel and railroad station—and came to the armory gate, where Daniel Whelan, second watchman, was taken prisoner. Brown's men forced the lock on the gate with the crowbar: the U.S. Armory at Harper's Ferry had fallen to the Provisional Army.

Brown, to Whelan and Williams:

> I came from Kansas, and this is a slave State: I want to free all the negroes in this State; I have possession now of the United States armory, and if the citizens interfere with me I must only burn the town and have blood.

Meanwhile, a raiding party was on its way up Bolivar Heights. Five miles from the Ferry lived Colonel Lewis W. Washington, great-grandnephew of the president, and possessor of a pistol presented to Washington by Lafayette, as well as a sword, reported to be a gift of Frederick the Great to the first president. Colonel Washington was awakened at midnight by four armed men and taken prisoner. The sword was secured and the colonel was led out to his carriage, behind which stood a farm wagon, with his liberated slaves. The party headed for the Ferry.

1:25 A.M., the B & O night express, Wheeling to Baltimore, arrived at the Wager House on schedule. After the usual stop the engineer started to cross the bridge, but was driven back to the station by gunfire.

Shephard Hayward, free Negro, merely passing by, was shot and killed, when he refused a command to halt.

At dawn, Brown permitted the train to go through. The engineer took it across the bridge and down the line to Monocacy, arriving at 7:05 A.M. Here the telegraph wires were intact, and the alarm was spread.

Brown ordered breakfast for forty-five, sent over from the Wager House. He himself refused to eat, fearing the food had been poisoned.

As the morning shift of workers arrived at the gates, they were taken hostage with the others.

Throughout the morning, Kagi kept urging Brown to escape while escape was possible, but Brown waited, for word of the expected slave uprising.

12 noon: the Jefferson guards reached the Maryland end of the Potomac bridge, drove back Brown's guard, and crossed to the Wager House. There was sporadic brutal street fighting during the day, but the militia was generally ineffective. Most of them were drunk.

Brown retired with his men and eleven of the most prominent
prisoners, including Colonel Washington, to the engine house. At
one point, Brown offered to surrender, on his own terms:

> In consideration of all my men, whether living or dead, or
> wounded, being soon safely in and delivered up to me at this
> point with all their arms and ammunition, we will then take our
> prisoners and cross the Potomac bridge, a little beyond which
> we will set them at liberty; after which we can negotiate about
> the Government property as may be best.

Terms were rejected, and men and hostages spent a second night in
the engine house, without food, shivering in the cold, unable to
sleep. Brown's son Oliver had been wounded.

Allstead, a prisoner:

> In the quiet of the night, young Oliver Brown died. He had
> begged again and again to be shot, in the agony of his wound,
> but his father had replied to him, "oh you will get over it," and,
> "If you must die, die like a man." Oliver lay quietly in a corner.
> His father called to him, after a time. No answer. "I guess he is
> dead," said Brown.

The second night, October 17, Brevet-Colonel Robert E. Lee, Second United States Cavalry, and First Lieutenant J. E. B. Stuart, First
Cavalry, attended a conference at the White House with the president
and secretary of war, and then arrived at Harper's Ferry to take
command of a detachment of U.S. Marines—who replaced the
drunken militia.

Stuart:

> By two A.M., Colonel Lee communicated to me his determi-
> nation to demand a surrender of the whole party at first dawn,
> and in case of refusal, which he expected, he would have ready a
> few picked men, who were at a signal to take the place at once

with the bayonet. He chose to demand a surrender before attacking, because he wanted every chance to save the prisoners unhurt, and to attack with bayonets for the same reason.

Through Stuart, Lee offered his terms to Brown:

Colonel Lee, United States army, commanding the troops sent by the President of the United States to suppress the insurrection at this place, demands the surrender of the persons in the armory buildings.

If they will peaceably surrender themselves and restore the pillaged property, they shall be kept in saftey to await the orders of the President. Colonel Lee represents to them, in all frankness, that it is impossible for them to escape; that the armory is surrounded on all sides by troops; and that if he is compelled to take them by force he cannot answer for their safety.

R. E. LEE
Colonel Commanding United States Troops.

Brown and Stuart parleyed at the engine house door for some minutes, but could not agree. Stuart gave the signal, and a storming detail of twelve men, under Lieutenant Green, battered down the door. Shots were fired, and there were casualties on both sides, but Brown and his men were easily subdued.

Green:

. . . the sorriest lot of people I ever saw. They had been without food for over sixty hours, in constant dread of being shot, and were huddled up in the corner where lay the body of Brown's son and one or two others of the insurgents who had been killed.

The attack was over.

---

Richard Realf, Brown's secretary of state:

[Brown believed that] upon the first intimation of a plan formed for the liberation of the slaves, they would immediately rise all

over the Southern States. He supposed that they would come
into the mountains to join him, where he proposed to work,
and that by flocking to his standard they would enable him (by
making the line of mountains which cuts diagonally through
Maryland and Virginia down through the Southern States into
Tennessee and Alabama, the base of his operations) to act upon
the plantations on the plains lying on each side of that range of
mountains, and that we should be able to establish ourselves in
the fastnesses, and if any hostile action (as would be) were taken
against us, either by the militia of the separate states or by the
armies of the United States, we proposed to defeat first the
militia, and next, if it were possible, the troops of the United
States, and then organize the freed blacks under this provisional
constitution, which would carve out for the locality of its
jurisdiction all that mountainous region in which the blacks
were to be established and in which they were to be taught the
useful and mechanical arts, and to be instructed in all the business
of life. Schools were also to be established, and so on. That was
it. . . . The negroes were to constitute the soldiers. John Brown
expected that all the free negroes in the Northern States would
immediately flock to his standard. He expected that all the slaves
in the Southern States would do the same. He believed, too,
that as many of the free negroes in Canada as could accompany
him, would do so.

One of the raiders, Charles Tidd, made his escape through the hills,
and eventually to Massachusetts. He reported that "twenty-five men
in the mountains of Virginia could paralyse the whole business of the
South, and nobody could take them."

Brown:

These mountains are the basis of my plan. God has given the
strength of the hills to freedom; they were placed here for the
emancipation of the negro race; they are full of natural forts,
where one man for defence will be equal to a hundred for attack;
they are also full of good hiding-places, where large numbers of
brave men could be concealed, and baffle and elude pursuit for a

long time. I know these mountains well, and could take a body
of men into them and keep them there, despite of all the efforts
of Virginia to dislodge them.

Thomas Wentworth Higginson:

> There was indeed, always a sort of thrill in John Brown's voice
> when he spoke of mountains. I shall never forget the quiet way
> in which he once told me that "God had established the Alle-
> ghany Mountains from the foundation of the world that they
> might one day be a refuge for fugitive slaves."

---

John Murray Forbes:

> Captain Brown was a grim, farmer-like looking man, with a
> long gray beard and glittering, gray-blue eyes which seemed to
> me to have a little touch of insanity about them.

Brown:

> I may be very insane, and I am so, if insane at all. But if that be
> so, insanity is like a very pleasant dream to me.

Henry A. Wise, governor of Virginia:

> And they are themselves mistaken who take him to be a mad-
> man. He is a bundle of the best nerves I ever saw. . . . He is cool,
> collected and indomitable, and it is but just to him to say that he
> was humane to his prisoners. . . . He is a fanatic, vain and
> garrulous, but firm, truthful and intelligent.

---

Brown, to his jailor:

> Have you any objection to my writing to my wife to tell her that
> I am to be hanged on the 2d of December at noon?

From his letters:

> *Dear Wife and Children, every one,—* . . . I can trust God with
> both the time and the manner of my death, believing, as I now
> do, that for me at this time to seal my testimony for God and
> humanity with my blood will do vastly more toward advancing
> the cause I have earnestly endeavored to promote, than all I have
> done in my life before.
>
> I feel no consciousness of guilt in the matter. . . . Already dear
> friends at a distance, with kindest sympathy, are cheering me
> with the assurance that posterity, at least, will do me justice.

Following sentencing, and before execution, at Charlestown, there
were constant rumors of invasion, of attempts to free him by force.

> Alarms would be given, the troops would fall into rank, and the
> cavalry would clatter out of town on some wild-goose chase.
> Night after night mysterious fires from burning barns or hay-
> stacks lighted up the sky, making the perturbed citizens believe
> that the rescue attack had come at last. The fires were never
> explained; perhaps the slaves did set them, as was generally
> believed.

December 2:

> As he came out the six companies of infantry and one troop of
> horse, with General Taliaferro and his entire staff, were deploy-
> ing in front of the jail, whilst an open wagon with a pine box, in
> which was a fine oak coffin, was waiting for him.
>
>> Brown: "I had no idea that Governor Wise considered
>> my execution so important."
>
> Brown looked around and spoke to several persons he recog-
> nized, and, walking down the steps, took a seat on the coffin
> box along with the jailor, Avis. He looked with interest on the

fine military display. . . . The wagon moved off, flanked by two files of riflemen in close order.

> Brown: "This *is* a beautiful country. I never had the pleasure of seeing it before."

On reaching the field where the gallows was erected, the prisoner said, "Why are none but military allowed in the inclosure? I am sorry citizens have been kept out." On reaching the gallows he observed Mr. Hunter and Mayor Green standing near, to whom he said, "Gentlemen, good-bye," his voice not faltering.

The prisoner walked up the steps firmly, and was the first man on the gallows. Avis and Sheriff Campbell stood by his side, and after shaking hands and bidding them an affectionate adieu, he thanked them for their kindness, when the cap was put over his face and the rope around his neck. Avis asked him to step forward on the trap. He replied, "You must lead me; I cannot see." The rope was adjusted, and the military order given, "Not ready yet!" The soldiers marched, countermarched, and took up position as if an enemy were in sight, and were thus occupied for nearly ten minutes, the prisoner standing all the time. . . .

He was swung off at fifteen minutes past eleven. A slight grasping of the hands and twitching of the muscles were seen.

> As the trap was sprung, a private of the Richmond Grays turned pale, his knees weak. Those near him asked if he felt ill, and he asked for a stiff drink of whiskey . . . It was John Wilkes Booth, who had come along for the show . . .

Then all was quiet.

The body was several times examined, and the pulse did not cease until thirty-five minutes had passed.

Colonel William T. Sherman, U.S.A.:

The march demonstrated the general laxity of discipline; for with all my personal efforts I could not prevent the men from straggling for water, blackberries or anything on the way they fancied.

Our men had been told at home that all they had to do was to make a bold appearance, and the Rebels would run.

General Beauregard, C.S.A.:

Of the topographical features of the country thus occupied it must suffice to say that Bull Run is a small stream, running in this locality nearly from west to east, to its confluence with the Occoquan River, about twelve miles from the Potomac, and draining a considerable scope of country from its source in Bull Run Mountain to a short distance of the Potomac Occoquan. At this season habitually low and sluggish, it is, however, rapidly and frequently swollen by the summer rains until unfordable. The banks for the most part are rocky and steep, but abound in long-used fords. The country on either side, much broken and thickly wooded, becomes gently rolling and open as it recedes from the stream. . . .

In view of these palpable military conditions, by 4:30 A.M. on the 21st of July [1861], I had prepared and dispatched orders directing the whole of the Confederate forces within the lines of Bull Run, including the brigades and regiments of General Johnston, which had arrived at that time, to be held in readiness to march at a moment's notice.

———————

. . . The Stone Bridge on the Confederate left was held by Evans with 1 regiment and Wheat's special battalion of infantry, 1 battery of 4 guns, and 2 companies of cavalry.

About 5:15 a.m., Tyler's artillery [Union] opened fire across the Stone Bridge and his infantry deployed over the open farm lands, with Schenck's brigade below and opposite to the bridge, and Keyes' and Sherman's brigades above it.

Beauregard:

As the Federalists had advanced with an extended line of skirmishers in front of Evans, that officer promptly threw forward the two flank companies of the Fourth South Carolina Regiment and one company of Wheat's Louisiana Battalion, deployed as skirmishers to cover his small front. An occasional scattering fire resulted, and thus the two armies in that quarter remained for more than an hour, while the main body of the enemy was marching his devious way through the Big Forest to take our forces in the flank and rear. . . .

A fierce and destructive conflict now ensued. The fire was withering on both sides, while the enemy swept our short thin lines with their numerous artillery.

> "George Knoll . . . being in his characteristic mood, but hungry, took from his haversack a chunk of fat bacon, stuffing himself while the artillery fire was in progress."

Beauregard:

Now, however, with the surging mass of over 14,000 Federal infantry pressing on their front, and under the incessant fire of at least twenty pieces of artillery, with the fresh brigades of Sherman and Keyes approaching, the latter already in musket range, our lines gave back. . . .

Fully conscious of this portentous disparity of force, as I posted the lines for the encounter, I sought to infuse into the hearts of my officers and men the confidence and determined spirit of resistance to this wicked invasion of the homes of a free people which I felt.

Now, full 2 o'clock P.M., I gave the order for the right of my line, except for my reserves, to advance to recover the plateau. It was done with uncommon resolution and vigor, and at the same time Jackson's brigade pierced the enemy's center with the determination of veterans and the spirit of men who fought for a sacred cause. . . . With equal spirit the other parts of the line made the onset and the Federal lines were broken and swept back at all points from the open ground of the plateau. Rallying soon, however, as they were strongly re-enforced by fresh regiments, the Federalists returned, and by weight of numbers pressed our lines back, recovered their ground and guns and renewed the offensive.

. . . About 3:30 P.M., the enemy, driven back on their left and center, and brushed from the woods bordering the Sudley Road, south and west of the Henry house, had formed a line of battle of truly formidable proportions, of crescent outline. . . .

But as Early formed his line and Beckham's pieces played upon the right of the enemy, Elzey's brigade, Gibbon's Tenth Virginia, Lieutenant-Colonel Stewart's First Maryland, and Vaughn's Third Tennessee regiments, Cash's Eighth and Kershaw's Second South Carolina, Wither's Eighteenth and Preston's Twenty-eighth Virginia advanced in an irregular line, almost simultaneously, with great spirit, from their several positions on the front and flanks of the enemy in their quarter of the field. At the same time, too, Early resolutely assailed their right flank and rear. Under this combined attack the enemy was soon forced, first, over the narrow plateau in the southern angle, made by the two roads so often mentioned, into a patch of woods on its western slope, thence back over Young's Branch and the turnpike into the fields of the Dogan farm and rearward, in extreme disorder, in all available directions toward Bull Run.

General Irwin McDowell, commanding U.S. forces:

But our men, exhausted with the fatigue and thirst, and confused by firing into each other, were attacked by the enemy's reserves, and driven from the position we had gained, overlooking Manassas. After this, the men could not be rallied.

Colonel Andrew Porter, Sixteenth U.S. Infantry:

Soon the slopes behind us were swarming with our retreating and disorganized forces, whilst riderless horses and artillery teams ran furiously through the flying crowd. All further efforts were futile; the words, gestures and threats of our officers were thrown away upon men who had lost all presence of mind and only longed for absence of body.

W. W. Blackford, Confederate officer:

The whole field was a confused swarm of men, like bees, running away as fast as their legs could carry them, with all order and organization abandoned. In a moment more the valley was filled with them as far as the eye could reach. They plunged through Bull Run wherever they came to it regardless of fords or bridges, and there many drowned. Muskets, cartridge boxes, belts, knapsacks, haversacks and blankets were thrown away in their mad race, that nothing might impede their flight. In the reckless haste the artillery drove over every one who did not get out of their way. Ambulance and wagon drivers cut the traces and dashed off on the mules.

General McDowell:

> The men having thrown away their haversacks in the battle and left them behind, they are without food; have eaten nothing since breakfast. We are without artillery ammunition. The larger part of the men are a confused mob, entirely demoralized.

John O. Casler, Confederate soldier:

> I saw three horses galloping off, dragging a fourth, which was dead.

William Howard Russell, reporter for the London *Times:*

> The scene on the road had now assumed an aspect which has not a parallel in any description I have ever read. Infantry soldiers on mules and draft horses, with the harness clinging to their heels, as much frightened as their riders; Negro servants on their masters' chargers; ambulances crowded with unwounded soldiers; wagons swarming with men who threw out the contents in the road to make room, grinding through a shouting, screaming mass of men on foot, who were literally yelling with rage at every halt.

A member of the Washington Artillery of New Orleans reported, after the battle:

> We live splendidly: Chicken, eggs, vegetables, milk, ice, and claret, paté de fois gras, sardines, etc.

---

Blackford:

> Along a shady little valley through which our road lay the surgeons had been plying their vocation all the morning upon the wounded. Tables about breast high had been erected upon which screaming victims were having legs and arms cut off. The surgeons and their assistants, stripped to the waist and all

bespattered with blood, stood around, some holding the poor fellows while others, armed with long bloody knives and saws, cut and sawed away with frightful rapidity, throwing the mangled limbs on a pile near by as soon as removed. Many were stretched on the ground awaiting their turn, many more were arriving continually, either limping along or borne on stretchers, while those upon whom operations had already been performed calmly fanned the flies from their wounds.

D. E. Johnston, Confederate soldier:

Returning to the battle line, we found ourselves groping around in the dark. . . . The cries of the Federal wounded, and the groans of the dying, the occasional volleys of musketry fired by some of our troops at imaginary foes, with the hooting of owls, made the night hideous and weird.

General McDowell, reporting from Fairfax Country Courthouse the following day:

I learn from prisoners that we are to be pressed here to-night and tomorrow morning, as the enemy's force is very large and they are elated. I think we heard cannon on our rear guards. I think now, as all my commanders thought at Centreville, there is no alternative but to fall back to the Potomac.

And another voice:

The defeated troops commenced pouring into Washington over the Long Bridge at daylight on Monday, 22d—day drizzling all through with rain. The Saturday and Sunday of the battle (20th, 21st) had been parched and hot to an extreme—the dust, the grime and smoke, in layers, sweated in, follow'd by other layers again sweated in, absorb'd by those excited souls—their clothes all saturated with the clay-powder filling the air—stirr'd up everywhere on the dry roads and trodden fields by the regi-

ments, swarming wagons, artillery, etc.—all the men with this
coating of murk and sweat and rain, now recoiling back, pouring over the Long Bridge—a horrible march of twenty miles,
returning to Washington baffled, humiliated, panic-struck.

. . . Sidewalks of Pennsylvania Avenue, Fourteenth street,
etc., crowded, jamm'd with citizens, darkies, clerks, every-
body, lookers-on; women in the windows, curious expressions
from faces. . . . During the forenoon, Washington gets all over
motley with these defeated soldiers—queer-looking objects,
strange eyes and faces, drench'd (the steady rain drizzles on all
day) and fearfully worn, hungry, haggard, blister'd in the
feet. . . . Amid the deep excitement, crowds and motion, and
desperate eagerness, it seems strange to see many, very many,
of the soldiers sleeping—in the midst of all, sleeping sound.
They drop down anywhere, on the steps of houses, up close by
the basements of fences, on the sidewalk, aside on some vacant
lot, and deeply sleep. A poor seventeen or eighteen year old boy
lies there, on the stoop of a grand house; he sleeps so calmly, so
profoundly. Some clutch their muskets.

Walt Whitman

September 24, 1861, at Hanging Rocks on North River—a branch
of Cacapon:

. . . The Confederates on the cliffs, rolled stones down upon the
advancing Union forces on the road below, and routed them.

On the Potomac, October 21, 1861:

> Harrison's is one of a number of long narrow islands. . . . It is
> nearly half a mile wide, and more than two miles in length. . . .
> Opposite the island, the Virginia shore rises abruptly; in many
> places directly from the water's edge, in cliffs or bluffs.

> [Union] General Stone ordered a reconnaissance by a few men
> from the force on Harrison's Island, which was opposite the
> high bluff at Ball's Bluff. They crossed in the moonlight, ad-
> vanced a short distance, and retired, reporting to General Stone
> that they had discovered a Rebel camp, which afterwards
> proved to be merely openings in an orchard, which looked to
> their excited eyes like tents. However, the camp was taken for
> granted, and . . . about 450 men were sent to capture it.

> The river was swollen and the current rapid, and there was
> much labor and delay in making use of the boats.

> To convey his battalion to the foot of the bluffs Colonel Devens
> had one four-oared bateau or "flat boat", and a couple of small
> skiffs, needing frequent bailing. . . . One or two other skiffs
> were subsequently added, but the transportation was wholly
> inadequate.

> The place for landing upon the Virginia shore was most unfor-
> tunately selected, being at a point where the shore rose with

great abruptness . . . and was studded with trees, being entirely impassable to artillery or infantry in line. . . . In fact, no more unfortunate position could have been forced upon us by the enemy for making an attack, much less selected by ourselves.

The bank is of a miry clay, and the heights almost precipitous, with fallen trees and rocks, making it very difficult to get up the artillery. Arriving by circuitous routes on the summit, we found an open field of six acres, covered with wild grass, scrub oak, and locust trees, and forming a segment of a circle, the arc of which was surrounded with trees.

The Federal position at this time was upon the plateau of the bluff, some 700 yards in front of the river, where there was a cleared field of ten or twelve acres.

. . . formed at the top of the Bluff, afterwards moving forward on the right, where they encountered the picket reserve of the enemy . . .

Colonel Baker . . . brought battalions . . . to reinforce our line, and under direct orders from General Stone, assumed command of the movement.

Lieutenant Bramhall, New York Light Artillery:

I crossed with the first piece . . . arriving upon the island after a half hour's hard labor to keep the boat from floating down the stream. We ascended the steep bank, made soft and sloppy by the passage of the troops, and at a rapid gait crossed the island to the second crossing. At this point we found only a scow, on which we did not dare to cross the piece and the horses together, and thus lost further time by being obliged to make two crossing. Upon arriving on the Virginia shore we were compelled to dismount the piece and carriage and haul the former up by the prolonge, the infantry assisting in carrying the parts of the latter to a point about thirty feet up a precipitous ascent, rendered almost impassable with soft mud, where we remounted the piece, and hitching up the horses dragged it through a perfect thicket up to the open ground above where the fighting was going on.

We had seen but little of the enemy during the day, as they were in the woods while our line was in the open, but they had, nevertheless, very seriously made known their presence to us. We were too ignorant to attempt any sort of cover.

The Virginians and Mississippians being accustomed to the rifle, most of them old hunters, rarely missed their man. Climbing into the tops of trees, creeping through the tall grass, or concealed in the gullies, they plied their weapons with murderous havoc especially among the Federal officers.

By this time there were many dead and wounded, and we used the boats to send them over to the Island. The cannons were useless—since the ammunition was exhausted, and the cannoneers killed or wounded. . . . The strength of the forces engaged was about 1600 Federals, against 3200 Confederates. Had there been proper transportation, this difference would have been remedied.

The re-enforcements from the island came up very slowly, and it was evident to all that unless aid in force reached us from the left, we should be driven into the river, as the increasing yells and firing of the enemy indicated their larger number.

. . . a wild, terror stricken yell; then the simultaneous crash of 1,000 muskets, each hurling its leaden contents along the Federal left and centre!

> Colonel W. H. Jenifer, CSA: "I sent my adjutant to you for ammunition and provisions, and if provisions could not be had at once, to send a barrel of whiskey."

Seeing that the crisis was come—as the Confederates were assuming the offensive and closing upon him from three sides, with the river at his back—Colonel Baker turned to the bayonet as the last hope. . . . Baker ran forward and at once received a stinging wound. . . .

At this moment the hostile lines were within stone's throw, and both advancing. The Federals, seeing the fall of their leader, halted. Some soldiers seized Baker's body and ran with it rearward. This started the rest.

> "Between the physical fear of going forward and the moral fear of turning back, there is a predicament of exceptional awkwardness. . . ."

. . . A general retreat took place. . . . All regimental order was lost, and the huddling of the men on the hill rendered the Confederate fire, which was rapidly closing in on all sides, so much the more fatal.

Brigadier General N. G. Evans, CSA:

At about 6 o'clock p.m. I saw that my command had driven the enemy near the banks of the Potomac. I ordered my entire force to charge and drive him into the river. The charge was immediately made by the whole command, and the forces of the enemy completely routed, and cried out for quarter along his whole line.

In this charge the enemy were driven back at the point of the bayonet, and many were killed and wounded by this formidable weapon.

Lieutenant Colonel John McGuirk, Seventeenth Mississippi Infantry:

Above the roar of musketry was heard the command of Colonel Featherston, "Charge, Mississippians, charge! Drive them into the Potomac or into eternity!" The sound of his voice seemed to echo from the vales of Maryland. The line arose as one man from a kneeling position, discharged a deadly volley, advanced the crescent line, and thus encircled the invaders.

Again, the Union side:

A kind of shiver ran through the huddled mass upon the brow
of the cliff; it gave way; rushed a few steps; then, in one wild,
panic-stricken herd, rolled, leaped, tumbled over the precipice!
The descent is nearly perpendicular, with ragged, jutting
crags. . . . Screams of pain and terror filled the air. Men seemed
suddenly bereft of reason; they leaped over the bluff with
muskets still in their clutch, threw themselves into the river
without divesting themselves of their heavy accoutrements—
hence went to the bottom like lead. Others sprung down upon
the heads and bayonets of those below.

The scow, which had already carried over many wounded, now
started on her last trip, but when starting, a number of uninjured
men rushed forward, disturbing the trim of the boat, so that
half way across the river she rolled over, and all were thrown
out. Only one man is known to have escaped drowning. The
scow floated down the stream and was lost. The small boats
were riddled by bullets and disappeared.

Lieutenant Bramhall, artillery:

Finding that the battle was lost to us, and with but one man left
to aid me . . . and growing weak and stiff from my wounds . . .
I caused the piece to be drawn down to the edge of the cliff,
whence it was afterward thrown down, lodging in the rocks
and logs with which the descent was cumbered. . . . The horses
belonging to the piece were all shot, . . . five of them lay dead
in one heap.

One year later:

We have been to Harrison Island, and in sight of Ball's Bluff,
which rested as quiet and silently as though blood had not dyed
its soil. We have countermarched, and our division is near the

Potomac. . . . A little fire is burning a few feet before me, and the smoke curls up lazily in the sunshine. The air has the lovely, dreamy haze of autumn. The trees are gently shaking off the ripe leaves. The hum of insects is not yet ended. Near are the strokes of our woodcutters axes. Farther off is the murmur of a rapid.

The Second Massachusetts Infantry, on the Masanutten Range, May 1862:

We climbed the hill. There was no *hard* climbing, however. The road over the gap was as smooth and firm as any in Roxbury or Dorchester. . . . Another brigade was bivouacked for a mile or two by the road, and their brilliant fires crackling all along on either side . . . made a bewildering and fascinating scene. At the top we rested, and turning to look, beheld a view of the utmost beauty; a lovely valley, of great breadth, confined by the distant Alleghanies, whose tops the rising sun was just tingeing. . . .

Then we returned. Up the hill and down again, and back to camp. On the way up, a few of us took short cuts from angle to angle once or twice to gather wild flowers. There was great abundance of several kinds. Wild cherry was in blossom, and laurel, and what they call dogwood here, which I think is found in Milton, in Massachusetts, and "red bud", without leaves, but gorgeous in its wealth of flowering; and of lowlier plants, the red columbine, mayflower, much like the New Hampshire one, which is more beautiful than that in the Plymouth woods (I have gathered both), the anemone, the iris, far more delicately lovely than any I ever saw wild before; and above all, such profusion of wood violets as one rarely finds, of which many were colored so like pansies that they were easily mistaken for them at a little distance. Sitting upon a rock to rest, the sight of belted men, with swords in their side and pistols ready, gathering flowers, awakened strange sensations.

## THE MARYLAND CAMPAIGN,
### SEPTEMBER 3 TO 20, 1862
### INCLUDING THE BATTLES OF
### SOUTH MOUNTAIN, CRAMPTON'S GAP AND ANTIETAM,
### OR SHARPSBURG.
#### BY
#### GENERAL ROBERT E. LEE
Commanding the Army of Northern Virginia
*Headquarters,* October—, 1862

Not to permit the season for active operations to pass without endeavoring to inflict injury upon the enemy, the best course appeared to be the transfer of the army into Maryland. Although not properly equipped for invasion, lacking much of the material of war, and feeble in transportation, the troops poorly provided with clothing, and thousands of them destitute of shoes, it was yet believed to be strong enough to detain the enemy upon the northern frontier until the approach of winter.

The Confederates forded the Potomac at Botoler's or Blackford's ford, below Shepherdstown, "where the river, from the wash of the dam above, was broad, sandy, and shallow."

On the 3d of September we marched with three days rations and bivouacked at Dranesville, with the whole army. The order was given on the following day for Jackson to cross the Potomac. . . .

On the 5th we marched through Leesburg and bivouacked in a half mile of the Potomac, which stream was next morning crossed.

As full of hope as the soldiers of Hannibal going over the Alps . . . the men splashed through the water, too happy to be moving forward to trouble themselves about wet clothing. . . .

It was with a deep heaving of the chest and expansion of the lungs with us all that we stood at last upon the Maryland shore. . . . At all of the farm houses near the river the people appeared hospitable and reb down to their boots, and crazy to see Lee. Adjutant Owen brought back a string of ladies, who overwhelmed the old man with kisses and welcomes.

The columns were soon upon the high road towards Boonesboro', and we were all struck with the beautiful scenery of this part of the country. As we climbed the hills long stretches of valley extended as far as the eye could reach in the direction of the Potomac. How still and peaceful it all looked.

Lee:

The arduous service in which our troops had been engaged, their great privations of rest and food, and the long marches without shoes over mountain roads, had greatly reduced our ranks before the action began. These causes had caused thousands of brave men to absent themselves.

E. P. Alexander, Confederate artillery officer:

About one-half of the small-arms were still the old smoothbore muskets of short range, and our rifled cannon ammunition was always inferior in quality. The lack of shoes was deplorable, and barefoot men with bleeding feet were no uncommon sight. Of clothing, our supply was so poor that it seemed no wonder the Marylanders held aloof from our shabby ranks. For rations, we were indebted mostly to the fields of roasting ears, and to the apple orchards. . . . On Sept. 5 the army began to cross the Potomac.

---

W. M. Owen, Confederate officer:

We reached the vicinity of Sharpsburg early in the morning of September 15, and formed a line of battle along the range of hills between the town and the stream, with our back to the Potomac.

On the opposite shore of the Antietam the banks are quite steep and afford good position for artillery. All the batteries present were placed in position along the ridge. Longstreet said, "Put them all in, every gun you have, long range and short range."

A courier arrived in hot haste, with news that Jackson had captured Harpers Ferry. . . .

"This is indeed good news," said General Lee; "let it be announced to the troops;" and staff officers rode at full gallop down the line, and the announcement was answered by great cheering.

September 17:

The battle began with the dawn. Morning found both armies just as they had slept, almost close enough to look into each other's eyes. . . . A battery was almost immediately pushed forward beyond the central woods, over a plowed field, near the top of the slope where the cornfield began. On this open field, in the corn beyond, and in the woods which stretched forward into the broad fields, like a promontory into the ocean, were the hardest and deadliest struggles of the day.

Kyd Douglas, Confederate officer:

With me it was a fearful day—one I am not likely ever to forget. With two hundred pieces of artillery turned against us and pouring a continuous fire with fearful accuracy upon our guns as well as our line of battle, I need not explain that I had more work than play, more danger than glory. . . . My first horse, "Ashby", in his first battle, between fright and excitement was exhausted in a few hours; another and then another became necessary. The day was hot, the battle terrific while it lasted, the suspense racking, the anxiety intense.

John Dooley, Confederate soldier:

About 11 A.M. (I think) the enemy advanced upon our center. We have a good view of our batteries, and as line after line of the blue coats advance to the charge, our guns open at about two hundred yards' distance. . . . We can plainly see the earth as it is torn up and scattered wildly about in face of each successive line of infantry that marches up the slope. . . .

This was the finest sight we witnessed today.

Another:

From our position on the right we could not see the combatants, but could hear the crash of small arms and the wild rebel yell. As long as we could hear this yell we felt that things were going our way.

Dooley:

In the field below us the enemy are slowly but cautiously approaching, crouching low as they advance behind the undulating tracks in the rich meadows through which they are passing. From the numbers of their flags which are distinctly visible above the rising ground we judge them to be at least two thousand in number. As long as our little battery of two guns is served with tolerable precision the enemy, who appear to be new troops, do not dare to venture close or raise their heads. But in a few minutes the Yankee artillery, far superior to ours, dismounted one of our pieces, killed the horses; and the remaining gunner, fearing capture, hitched the only remaining horse to the other cannon and made away to the rear as hard as he could go.

I shall never forget poor Beckham on Kemper's staff. As soon as our first gun opened on the enemy, he gave a lusty cheer and rising in his stirrups flung his hat around his head, wild with enthusiasm. Almost instantly he was hurled from his horse by a shot and his foot terribly mangled. He was borne from the field cheering as he went.

The enemy having taken our position appeared to think they had performed wonders, for instead of pursuing us and shooting us down, they began to give regular *methodical* cheers, as if they had gained a game of base ball.

A soldier:

I recall a round shot that came ricochetting over the ground, cutting little furrows, tossing the earth into the air, as the plow of the locomotive turns its white furrow after a snowstorm. Its speed gradually diminished and a soldier was about to catch it, as if he were at a game of baseball.

General John B. Gordon, CSA:

The predicted assault came. The men in blue filed down the opposite slope, crossed the Antietam, and formed in my front, an assaulting column four lines deep. The brave Union Commander, superbly mounted, placed himself in front, while his band in rear cheered them with martial music. It was a thrilling spectacle. The entire force, I concluded, was composed of fresh troops. As we stood looking upon that brilliant pageant, I thought, "What a pity to spoil with bullets such a scene of martial beauty." But there was nothing else to do.

Every act of the Union commander clearly indicated his purpose to depend on bayonets. He essayed to break through by the momentum of his solid column. It was my business to prevent this. To oppose man against man and strength against strength was impossible; for there were four lines of blue to my one of gray. During the few minutes required for the column to reach my line, I could not hope to disable a sufficient number of the enemy to reduce his strength to an equality with mine. The only remaining plan was to hold my fire until the advancing Federals were almost upon my lines. I did not believe that any troops on earth, with empty guns in their hands, could withstand so sudden a shock. My men were at once directed to lie down upon the grass. Not a shot would be fired until my voice should be heard commanding "Fire!"

There was no artillery at this point upon either side, and not a rifle was discharged. The stillness was literally oppressive, as this column of Union infantry moved majestically toward us. Now the front rank was within a few rods of where I stood. With all my lung power I shouted "Fire!"

Our rifles flamed and roared in the Federals' faces like a blinding blaze of lightning. The effect was appalling. The entire front line, with few exceptions, went down. Before the rear lines could recover, my exultant men were on their feet, devouring them with successive volleys. Even then these stubborn blue lines retreated in fairly good order.

The fire now became furious and deadly. The list of the slain was lengthened with each passing moment. Near nightfall, the awful carnage ceased; Lee's center had been saved.

A North Carolina soldier:

The sun seemed almost to go backwards, and it appeared as if night would never come.

Major-General John G. Walker, CSA:

To those who have not been witnesses to a great battle like this, where more than a hundred thousand men, armed with all the appliances of modern science and skill, are engaged in the work of slaughtering each other, it is impossible by the power of words to convey an adequate idea of its terrible sublimity.

Douglas Southall Freeman:

Sharpsburg itself was aflame and under artillery fire; its side streets were filled with demoralized soldiers, who had become

separated from their commands; above it, through the smoke
and bursting shells, flocks of bewildered pigeons flew round
and round.

---

General Hood, CSA:

Whole ranks of brave men, whose deeds were unrecorded save
in the hearts of loved ones at home, were mowed down in
heaps to the right and left. Never before was I so continuously
troubled with fear that my horse would further injure some
wounded fellow soldier, lying helpless upon the ground.

General Hooker, USA:

I discovered that a heavy force of the enemy had taken possession
of a corn-field (I have since learned about a 30-acre field) in my
immediate front, and from the sun's rays falling on their bayonets projecting above the corn, could see that the field was filled
with the enemy with arms in their hands. . . . In the time I am
writing every stalk of corn in the northern and greater part of
the field was cut as closely as could have been done with a knife,
and the slain lay in rows, precisely as they had stood in their
ranks a few moments before.

The poor fellow's whole lower jaw had been knocked off;
carrying tongue and teeth with it, leaving the moustache,
clotted with blood; arching over a frightful chasm of tangled
muscles and arteries! The dripping from the aperture ran down
over his bosom in a sheet of gelid, clotted gore.

Major-General McClellan, USA:

The enemy was pressed back to near the crest of the hill, where
he was encountered in great strength posted in a sunken road
forming a natural pit running in a northwesterly direction. . . .
Here a terrific fire of musketry burst from both lines.

A Union soldier:

> It seemed like merely a hop, skip, and jump till we were at the
> lane, and into it, the Confederate breaking away in haste and
> fleeing up the slope. What a sight was that lane! I shall not dwell
> on the horror of it; I saw many a ghastly array of dead afterward,
> but none, I think, that so affected me as did the sight of the poor
> brave fellows in butternut homespun that had there died.

George F. Noyes, Union officer:

> I was walking down the lines, when a regimental captain thus
> accosted me, holding up a great piece of pork on his sword:
> "Look here, captain, this is the allowance of pork for my com-
> pany, and I shall have to eat it all, for I am the only one left."

> As I rode past the barn, a collection of amputated limbs lying
> outside the door attested the hurried and wholesale character of
> the work going on within.

------

> . . . a fine horse struck with death at the instant when, cut down
> by his wound, he was attempting to rise from the ground. His
> head was half lifted, his neck proudly arched, every muscle
> seemed replete with animal life. . . .

> Near by stood a wounded battery-horse and a shattered caisson
> belonging to one of Hood's batteries. The animal had eaten
> every blade of grass within reach. No human being ever looked
> more imploringly for help than that dumb animal, wounded
> beyond the possibility of moving, yet resolutely standing, as if
> knowing that lying down would be the end.

> Behind the battery came hobbling as best they could a string of
> fearfully mutilated horses which had been turned loose as they
> received their wounds, and who had followed their comrades
> when they left the spot where they had been in action. After
> they had all passed, I saw a horse galloping after them and

dragging something. Thinking it was his rider as he emerged from the clouds of smoke on the field of battle, I moved to intercept and stop the animal, but to my horror discovered that the horse was dragging his own entrails from the gaping wound of a cannonball, and after passing us a few yards the poor brute fell dead with a piercing scream.

---

General Lee:

It was now nearly dark and the enemy had massed a number of batteries to sweep the approaches to the Antietam. . . . Our troops were much exhausted and greatly reduced in numbers by fatigue and the casualties of battle. Under these circumstances it was deemed injudicious to push our advantage further in the face of fresh troops of the enemy.

Douglas:

I went off the pike and was compelled to go through a field in the rear of Dunker Church, over which, to and fro, the pendulum of battle had swung several times that day. It was a dreadful scene, a veritable field of blood. The dead and dying lay as thick over it as harvest sheaves. The pitiable cries for water and appeals for help were much more horrible to listen to than the deadliest sounds of battle. Silent were the dead, and motionless. But here and there were raised stiffened arms; heads made a last effort to lift themselves from the ground; prayers were mingled with oaths, the oaths of delirium; men were wriggling over the earth; and midnight hid all distinction between the blue and the gray. My horse trembled under me in terror, looking down at the ground, sniffing the scent of blood, stepping falteringly as a horse will over or by the side of human flesh; afraid to stand still, hesitating to go on, his animal instinct shuddering at this cruel human mystery. Once his foot slid into a little shallow filled with blood and spurted a little stream on his legs and boots. . . . I dismounted and giving the reins to my courier I started on foot.

Noyes:

It is a narrow country lane, hollowed out somewhat between the fields, partially shaded. . . Here they stood in line of battle. . . . In every attitude conceivable—some piled in groups of five or six; some grasping their muskets . . . ; some, evidently officers, killed while encouraging their men; some lying in the position of calm repose, all black and swollen, and ghastly with wounds.

The air grows terribly offensive from the unburied bodies; and a pestilence will speedily be bred if they are not put under ground. The most of the Union soldiers are now buried, though some only slightly.

The men were now permitted to bring in bundles of straw from the neighboring farms, with which they made themselves beds, and lay down in line of battle; the tired gunners made themselves similarly comfortable alongside their guns. . . . No one removed even his sword; our horses stood saddled and ready. . . .
There was no tree over our heads to shut out the stars.

---

Casualties at Antietam, killed and wounded: 23,000. . .

---

Noyes—September 18, the following day:

The feeling seemed to possess every heart that this day was to be crowned with victory; the whole tone of conversation as we drank our coffee on the grass was hopeful, nay, almost exultant; the hour for crushing the rebellion seemed to have struck; the opportunity had come to drive the rebels into the Potomac. . . .
But sunrise came, hour after hour slipped by, with no orders to advance . . . and gradually a bitter feeling began to trouble us, while the conviction forced itself upon our minds that the enemy was to be permitted to escape.

September 19:

> Up again at 3 A.M., we drank our coffee, saw that the division
> had a good breakfast, and made all ready for battle. . . . Finally,
> at 8 A.M., we learned that the rebels had slipped through our
> fingers and returned across the Potomac. The river, lately in
> their rear, and forming one side of the angle into which we had
> driven them, was now their best defense against us.
>     . . . The campaign must now be transferred to Virginia; the
> long, weary days of marching and nights of shelterless discom-
> fort were all to be again endured.

Douglas:

> On the night of the 18th the Confederate army crossed into
> Virginia at Blackford's Ford, even taking its debris with it, all
> its wagons and guns, useless wagons, disabled guns, every-
> thing. If a scavenger had gone over the field the next day, he
> would have found nothing worth carrying off. General Lee
> watched this crossing, lasting through the night, and gave
> directions to facilitate it. General Jackson on horseback spent
> much of his time in the middle of the river, urging everything
> and everybody to push on.
>
> The scene on the Maryland side on the night of the crossing
> rivaled Bedlam. The wagon train had to go down a very high
> and almost perpendicular bank, and except for the still greater
> danger from behind, was such a descent as no prudent wagoner
> would ever have attempted to make. Although it was as precip-
> itous as the road to perdition, the teamsters had to make an
> elbow half way down, at the imminent risk of an overturn—
> some of the wagons actually meeting with such a calamity.
> These were set fire to, partly for warmth, partly for the purpose
> of seeing. . . .
>     The strangest feature of the whole affair, was the grotesque
> appearance of our army who had stripped off most of their
> clothes, and who went shuddering and shivering in the cold
> water. . . .

Artillery, infantry, ambulances, wagons, all mixed up in what appeared to be inextricable confusion in the water; and the ford, too, was full of large boulders. Immense fires were blazing on the banks, which had the effect of blinding both men and animals. Staff-officers stood on either bank, shouting to the drivers.

General Walker:

As I rode into the river, I passed General Lee, sitting on his horse in the stream, watching the crossing of the wagons and artillery. Returning my greeting, he inquired as to what was still behind. There was nothing but the wagons containing my wounded and a battery, all of which were near at hand, and I told him so,
"Thank God!" I heard him say as I rode on.

Reaching Virginia, many of the stragglers fled up the Shenandoah Valley, those who had shoes throwing them away as they ran, so they would not be reenlisted.

Col. Blackford, CSA, rode north with Jeb Stuart, June 1863,

crossing the Occoquan at Wolf Run Shoals, capturing a small
force at Fairfax Court House, passing through Dranesville, and
reaching Rowser's Ford of the Potomac on the night of the
twenty-seventh. The ford was wide and deep and might well
have daunted a less determined man, for the water swept over
the pommels of our saddles. To pass the artillery without wet-
ting the ammunition in the chests was impossible, provided it
was left in them, but Stuart had the cartidges distributed among
the horsemen and it was thus taken over in safety. The guns and
caissons went clean out of sight beneath the surface of the rapid
torrent, but all came out without the loss of a piece or a man,
though the night was dark, and by three o'clock in the morning
of the twenty-eighth of June we all stood wet and dripping on
the Maryland shore.

At another ford, R. A. Shotwell:

Thousands of rough voices sang . . . the musicians, nude as
Adam, each with a bundle of clothes on top of his head (to keep
them dry) tooting with "might and main" on their brass
horns. . . . Several columns crossing together, with colonels
on horseback, flags fluttering, and the forest of bright bayonets
glistening in the afternoon sun. . . .

---

Longstreet, addressing Lee, Gettysburg, July 1:

All we have to do is throw our army around by their left, and we shall interpose between the Federal army and Washington. We can get a strong position and wait. . . .

"No," said General Lee; "the enemy is there, and I am going to attack him there."

I suggested that such a move as I proposed would give us control of the roads leading to Washington and Baltimore, and reminded General Lee of our original plans. If we had fallen behind Meade and had insisted on staying between him and Washington, he would have been compelled to attack and would have been badly beaten. General Lee answered, "No; they are there in position, and I am going to whip them or they are going to whip me." I saw he was in no frame of mind to listen to further argument at that time, so I did not push the matter, but determined to renew the subject the next morning. It was then about 5 o'clock in the afternoon. . . .

When the battle of the 2d was over, General Lee pronounced it a success, as we were in possession of ground from which we had driven the Federals and had taken several field-pieces. The conflict had been fierce and bloody, and my troops had driven back heavy columns and had encountered a force three or four times their number, but we had accomplished little toward victorious results.

I was disappointed when he came to me on the morning of the 3d and directed that I should renew the attack against Cemetery Hill, probably the strongest point of the Federal line. For that purpose he had already ordered up Pickett's division. . . .

"I want you to take Pickett's division and make the attack. I will reenforce you by two divisions of the Third Corps."

"That will give me fifteen thousand men," I replied. "I have been a soldier, I may say, from the ranks up to the position I now hold. I have been in pretty much all kinds of skirmishes, from those of two or three soldiers up to those of an army corps, and

I think I can safely say there never was a body of fifteen thousand men who could make that attack successfully."

The general seemed a little impatient at my remarks, so I said nothing more. . . .

The plan of assault was as follows: our artillery was to be massed in a wood from which Pickett was to charge, and it was to pour a continuous fire upon the cemetery. Under cover of this fire and supported by it, Pickett was to charge.

---

A Confederate soldier:

The night before, when we had taken our place for bivouac on the corpse-covered battle field, there rose before us, what we at first thought was a cloud, black and threatening, but which we soon discovered were the mountains behind, or on which the Federal left was posted; protected, we discovered, too, on the morrow, by breastworks. In regarding this we stared at each other in amazement.

Lieutenant Haskell, USA:

The advantages of the position, briefly, were these: the flanks were quite well protected by the natural defenses there, Round Top up the left, and a rocky, steep untraversable ground up the right. Our line was more elevated than that of the enemy, consequently our artillery had a greater range and power than theirs. On account of the convexity of our line, every part of the line could be reinforced by troops having to move a shorter distance than if the line were straight; further, for the same reason, the line of the enemy must be concave, and, consequently, longer, and with an equal force, thinner, and so weaker than ours. Upon those parts of our line which were wooded, neither we nor the enemy could use artillery; but they were so strong by nature, aided by art, as to be readily defended by a small against a very large, body of infantry. When the line was open, it had the advantage of having open country in front, consequently, the enemy here could not surprise, as we were on

a crest, which besides the other advantages that I have mentioned, had this: the enemy must advance to the attack up an
ascent, and must therefore move slower, and be, before coming
to us, longer under our fire, as well as more exhausted. These,
and some other things, rendered our position admirable.

A Confederate, surveying the enemy positions:

His troops seemed to be heavily massed right on our only point
of attack. Holding an advanced front, almost inaccessible in the
natural difficulties of the ground, first by a line of skirmishers,
almost as heavy as a single line of battle, in the lower ground;
then the steep acclivity of the "Ridge" covered with two tiers of
artillery, and two lines of infantry supports. These had to be
passed over before reaching the crest of the heights where his
heavy reserves of infantry were massed in double column.

Colonel James Arthur Lyon Fremantle of His Majesty's Coldstream
Guards, attached to the Confederates as an observer:

Colonel Sorrell, the Austrian, and I arrived at 5 A.M. at the
same commanding position we were on yesterday, and I
climbed up a tree in company with Captain Schreibert of the
Prussion army. Just below us were seated Generals Lee, Hill,
Longstreet, and Hood, in consultation—the two latter assisting
their deliberations by the truly American custom of whittling.

Longstreet: "Never was I so depressed as that day."

_____

As early as three o'clock on the morning of the 3rd of July
Pickett's division was under arms and moving to the right and
southeast of the Cashtown and Gettysburg road.

. . . A shady, quiet march . . . we halted for a short time in the
woods, but moved forward pretty soon into a field, near a
branch.

Lieutenant Haskell, in the Union position:

Eleven o'clock came. The noise of battle has ceased upon the right; not a sound of a gun or musket can be heard on all the field; the sky is bright, with only the white fleecy clouds floating over from the west. The July sun streams down its fire upon the bright iron of the muskets in stacks upon the crest and the dazzling brass of the Napoleons. The Army lolls and longs for the shade. . . . The silence and sultriness of a July noon are supreme.

A Union soldier:

Shortly after eleven o'clock the firing ceased, and, for over an hour, there was hardly a picket shot heard. It was a queer sight to see men look at each other without speaking; the change was so great men seemed to go on tiptoe, not knowing how to act. . . . I began looking around for something to eat.

John Dooley:

While we are resting here we amuse ourselves by pelting each other with green apples.

A Confederate:

As the sun climbed towards the meridian, many of the men drew out their "corn dodgers" and bits of bacon, to make their frugal dinner. . . . Others spread their blankets on the gravelly hillside and stretched themselves for a nap. Everything looked quiet, dull and lazy,—as one sees the harvest-hands lolling under the trees at noontime.

Haskell:

We dozed in the heat, and lolled upon the ground, with half-open eyes. Our horses were hitched to the trees munching some oats. A great lull rests upon all the field. Time was heavy.

Fremantle:

> At noon all Longstreet's dispositions were made. His troops for attack were deployed into line, and lying down in the woods; his batteries were ready to open. The general then dismounted and went to sleep.

At General Meade's headquarters, there was not wanting to the peacefulness of the scene the singing of a bird, which had a nest in the peach tree.

---

General Alexander, CSA:

> I rode to see Pickett, who was with his division a short distance in the rear. . . . He seemed very sanguine, and thought himself in luck to have the chance. Then I felt that I could not make any delay or let the attack suffer by any indecision on my part. And, that General Longstreet might know my intention, I wrote him only this: "GENERAL: When our artillery fire is at its best, I shall order Pickett to charge."

Lieutenant Colonel W. M. Owen, CSA:

> The order to fire the signal-gun was immediately communicated . . . and the report of the first gun rang out upon the still summer air. There was a moment's delay with the second gun, a friction-primer having failed to explode. It was but a little space of time, but a hundred thousand men were listening. Finally a puff of smoke was seen at the Peach Orchard, then came a roar and a flash, and 138 pieces of Confederate artillery opened upon the enemy's position, and the deadly work began with the noise of the heaviest thunder.

Lieutenant Haskell:

> In an instant . . . the report of gun after gun in rapid succession smote our ears and their shells plunged down and exploded all

around us. We sprang to our feet. In briefest time the whole Rebel line to the West was pouring out its thunder and its iron upon our devoted crest. The wildest confusion for a few moments obtained sway among us. The shells came bursting all about. The servants ran terror-stricken for dear life and disappeared. The horses, hitched to the trees or held by the slack hands of the orderlies, neighed out in fright and broke away and plunged riderless through the fields.

And from soldiers on both sides:

The ground roar of nearly the whole artillery of both armies burst in on the silence, almost as suddenly as the full notes of an organ would fill a church.

The armies seemed like mighty wild beasts growling at each other.

The men did not cheer or shout—they growled.

We thought that at the second Bull Run, at the Antietam, and at Fredericksburg . . . we had heard heavy cannonading; they were but holiday salutes compared with this. Besides the great ceaseless roar of the guns, which was but the background of the others, a million various minor sounds engaged the ear. The projectiles shriek long and sharp. They hiss, they scream, they growl, they sputter; all sounds of life and rage; and each has its different note.

The enemy shot hurtled among us and clipped off the clover heads by our side.

The very earth shook as from a mighty quake. So intense were its vibrations that loose grass, leaves, and twigs arose from six to eight inches above the ground, hovered and quivered as birds about to drop.

Large limbs were torn from the trunks of the oak trees under which we lay and precipitated down upon our heads.

The sun . . . was now darkened. . . . . In any direction might be
seen guns, swords, haversacks, heads, limbs, flesh and bones in
confusion or dangling in the air or bounding on the earth.

A small boy of twelve years was riding with us at the time. This
urchin took a diabolical interest in the bursting of shells, and
screamed with delight when he saw them take effect.

Riderless horses galloping madly through the fields. . . . Mules
with ammunition, pigs wallowing about, cows in the pasture.

A shell at our right exploded, and a piece cut through the bowels
of the off wheel horse, another striking the nigh swing horse
. . . on the gambrel joint, breaking the off leg. . . . We continued on, the wheel horse trampling on his bowels all the time.

When the cannonade was at its height, a Confederate band of
music, between the cemetery and ourselves, began to play
polkas and waltzes, which sounded very curious.

Alfred B. Gardner was struck in the left shoulder, almost tearing
his arm from his body. He lived a few minutes and died shouting, "Glory to God! I am happy! Hallelujah!"

———————————

General Longstreet:

Unwilling to trust myself with the entire responsibility, I had
instructed Colonel Alexander to observe carefully the effect of
the fire upon the enemy and, when it began to tell, to notify
Pickett to begin the assault. I was so impressed with the hope-
lessness of the charge that I wrote the following note to Alexander:

"If the artillery fire does not have the effect to drive off the enemy
or greatly demoralize him, I would prefer that you should not
advise General Pickett to make the charge. I shall rely a great deal
on your judgement to determine the matter, and shall expect
you to let Pickett know when the moment offers."

To my note the colonel replied as follows:

"I will only be able to judge the effect of our fire upon the enemy by his return fire, for his infantry is but little exposed to view, and the smoke will obscure the whole field. If there is an alternative to this attack, it should be carefully considered before opening our fire, for it will take all the artillery ammunition we have left."

Alexander:

I was startled by the receipt of a note from Longstreet, ordering me to judge whether or not the attack should be made at all.

Until that moment, though I fully recognized the strength of the enemy's position, I had not doubted that we would carry it, in my confidence that Lee was ordering it. But here was a proposition that I should decide the question. Overwhelming reasons against the assault at once seemed to stare me in the face. . . .

Before the cannonade opened I had made up my mind to give Pickett the order to advance within fifteen or twenty minutes after it began. But when I looked at the full developement of the enemy's batteries, and knew that his infantry was generally protected from our fire by stone walls and swells of the ground, I could not bring myself to give the word. It seemed madness to launch infantry into that fire, with nearly three quarters of a mile to go at midday under a July sun. I let the 15 minutes pass, and 20, and 25, hoping vainly for something to turn up. . . .

The enemy's fire suddenly began to slacken. . . . I wrote Pickett, urgently: "For God's sake come quick. The eighteen guns are gone; come quick, or my ammunition won't let me support you properly."

Longstreet:

Pickett said, "General, shall I advance?"

The effort to speak the order failed, and I could only indicate it by an affirmative bow. He accepted the duty with seeming confidence of success, leaped on his horse, and rode gayly to his command. . . .

General Pickett, a graceful horseman, sat lightly in the saddle, his brown locks flowing quite over his shoulders.

Alexander:

Longstreet said, "I don't want to make this attack. I would stop it now but that General Lee ordered it and expects to go on. I don't see how it can succeed."

I listened, but did not dare offer a word. The battle was lost if we stopped. Ammunition was far too low to try anything else, for we had been fighting three days. There was a chance, and it was not my part to interfere. While Longstreet was still speaking, Pickett's division swept out of the wood and showed the full length of its grey ranks and shining bayonets, as grand a sight as ever a man looked on.

Colonel W. H. Taylor, CSA:

The charge was made down a gentle slope, and then up to the enemy's lines, a distance of over half a mile, denuded of forests, and in full sight of the enemy, and perfect range of their artillery.

And others:

Before us lay bright fields and fair landscape.

. . . a scene of unsurpassed grandeur and majesty. . . . As far as eye could reach could be seen the advancing troops, their gay war flags fluttering in the gentle summer breeze, while their sabers and bayonets flashed and glistened in the midday sun.

. . . here and there an officer motioning with his sword to perfect the alignment, which, as a general thing, is as fine as on a holiday parade.

In my admiration and enthusiasm I rushed some ten paces in advance and cast my eyes right and left. It was magnificent!

John Dooley:

I tell you, there is no romance in making one of these charges. . . . When you rise to your feet as we did today, I tell you the enthusiasm of ardent breasts in many cases *ain't there* and instead of burning to avenge the insults of our country, families and altars and firesides, the thought is most frequently, *Oh,* if I could just come out of this charge safely how thankful *would I be!*

A Confederate observer:

As Pickett's Division pressed on by us . . . the fixed look in their face, showed that they had steeled themselves to certain death.

General Franklin Sawyer, USA:

The front of the column was nearly up the slope . . . when suddenly a terrific fire from every available gun from the Cemetery to Round Top Mountain burst upon them. The distinct, graceful lines of the rebels underwent an instantaneous transformation. They were at once enveloped in a dense cloud of smoke and dust. Arms, heads, blankets, guns and knapsacks were thrown and tossed into the clear air. . . . A moan went up from the field, distinctly to be heard amid the storm of battle.

Lead and iron seemed to fill the air, as in a sleet storm . . .

Men, or fragments of men, were being thrown in the air every moment, but, closing up the gaps and leaving swaths of dead and dying in their tracks, these brave men still kept up their march.

Alexander:

> We were halted for a moment by a fence, and as the men threw
> it down for the guns to pass, I saw in one of the corners a man
> sitting down and looking up at me. A solid shot had carried
> away both jaws and his tongue. . . . He sat up and looked at me
> steadily.

Captain June Kimble, CSA:

> For five, perhaps ten minutes we held our ground and looked
> back for and prayed for support. It came not.

Alexander:

> Pickett's men never halted, but opened fire at close range,
> swarmed over the fences, and among the enemy's guns—were
> swallowed up in smoke, and that was the last of them. The
> conflict hardly seemed to last five minutes before they were
> melted away.

Longstreet:

> When the smoke cleared away, Pickett's Division was gone.
> Nearly two-thirds of his men lay dead on the field, and the
> survivors were sullenly retreating down the hill.

A Confederate:

> Amidst that still continuous, terrible fire, they slowly, sullenly,
> recrossed the plain—all that was left of them. . . .

Alexander:

> About that time General Lee, entirely alone, rode up and re-
> mained with me a long time. He then probably first appreciated
> the full extent of the disaster as the disorganized stragglers made

their way back to us. . . . But, whatever his emotions, there was no trace of them in his calm, self-possessed bearing.

Longstreet:

> There is no doubt that General Lee, during the crisis of that campaign, lost the matchless equipoise that characterized him, and that whatever mistakes were made were not so much matters of deliberate judgement as the impulses of a great mind disturbed by unparalleled conditions.

A Confederate:

> During the whole of this miserable day, and part of the preceding, the men had nothing to eat, and were very often without water. I succeeded at one time, in satisfying the pangs of hunger, by eating the fruit from a cherry tree, which either hung close to the ground, or whose boughs had been struck off by the bullets and shells.

Dooley:

> I begin now to suffer from thirst, for the only water they bring us is from a neighboring run which is warm and muddy and has the additional properties belonging to human blood and dead bodies.

> This is a horrid night. . . .

> Here is a poor wounded Confederate who is walking up and down, wandering anywhere his cracked brain directs him. Just on top of his head and penetrating to his brain is a large opening made by a shell in which I might insert my hand. He walks about as if nothing was the matter with him, and pays no attention to any advice given him.

Another victim and member of my regiment is deliriously moaning and shouting all the night. He begins in a low tone of voice and shouts louder and louder, using only one phrase all the time, until he becomes exhausted. Thus he repeats frantically a hundred times at least the words, "I'm proud I belong to the 1st Va. Regiment!"

------

Brigadier-General John D. Imobden, CSA, 1 A.M., July 4, the following morning:

When [General Lee] arrived there was not even a sentinal on duty at his tent, and no one of his staff was awake. The moon was high in the clear sky and the silent scene was unusually vivid. As he approached and saw us lying on the grass under a tree, he spoke, reined in his jaded horse, and essayed to dismount. The effort to do so betrayed so much physical exhaustion that I hurriedly rose and stepped forward to assist him, but before I reached his side he had succeeded in alighting, and threw his arm across the saddle to rest, and fixing his eyes upon the ground leaned in silence and almost motionless upon his equally weary horse,—the two forming a striking and never-to-be-forgotten group. The moon shone full upon his massive features and revealed an expression of sadness that I had never before seen upon his face.

Lee to Imboden, 2 A.M.:

We must now return to Virginia. As many of our poor wounded as possible must be taken home. I have sent for you, because your men and horses are fresh and in good condition, to guard and conduct our train back to Virginia. The duty will be arduous, responsible and dangerous.

July 4, noon:

The rain fell in blinding sheets; the meadows were soon overflowed, and fences gave way before the raging streams. During

the storm, wagons, ambulances, and artillery carriages by hun-
dreds—nay, by thousands—were assembling in the fields . . .
in one confused and apparently inextricable mass. As the afternoon wore on there was no abatement in the storm. . . . Horses
and mules were blinded and maddened by the wind and water.

Imboden, the night of the Fourth:

After dark I set out from Cashtown to gain the head of the
column during the night. My orders had been peremptory that
there should be no halt for any cause whatever. If an accident
should happen to any vehicle, it was immediately to be put out
of the road and abandoned. The column moved rapidly, consid-
ering the rough roads and the darkness. . . . For four hours I
hurried forward . . . and in all that time I was never out of the
hearing of the groans and cries of the wounded and dying.
Scarcely one in a hundred had received adequate surgical aid,
owing to the demands on the hard-working surgeons from still
worse cases that had to be left behind. Many of the wounded in
the wagons had been without food for thirty-six hours. Their
torn and bloody clothing, matted and hardened, was rasping
the tender, inflamed and still oozing wounds. Very few of the
wagons had even a layer of straw in them, and all were without
springs, . . . the teams trotted on, urged by whip and shout.

---

Alexander:

In order to protect his retreat, Lee had maintained a pontoon
bridge at Falling Waters, a few miles from Williamsport. But it
was weakly guarded, and on June 5 a small enemy raiding party
. . . had broken it and destroyed some boats, fortunately not
all. The retreat of the army was, therefore, brought to a standstill
just when forty-eight hours more would have placed it beyond
pursuit. We were already nearly out of provisions, and now the
army was about to be penned up on the riverbank and subjected
to an attack at his leisure by Meade.

All diligence was used to relieve the situation. The ferryboats were in use by day and by night carrying over, first, our wounded, and next, 5,000 Federal prisoners brought from Gettysburg. Warehouses on the canal were torn down, and from the timber new pontoon boats were being built to repair the bridge at Falling Waters.

A Confederate:

The river was full and past fording when we arrived at it, and the ferryboat was kept busy taking men across and bringing ammunition back for our army. The cavalry were swimming their horses across all the time we were at work, the army lying in line of battle, waiting for us to get the bridge built. . . . When the bridge was completed the army commenced crossing the river, but the bridge was kept full all the time with ambulances, medical wagons, ordnance wagons and artillery, and such things as had to be kept dry, consequently there was no room for the infantry to cross, except one division, that was guarding the bridge. The rest waded the river at Williamsport. The greater portion of the wagon train had to ford at the same place. The water came up under the arms of the men.

Blackford:

On either bank fires illuminated the scene, the water reached the armpits of the men and was very swift. By the bright lurid light the long line of heads and shoulders and the dim sparkling of their musket barrels could be traced across the watery space, dwindling away almost to a thread before it reached the further shore. The passage of the wagon trains was attended with some loss, for the current in some cases swept them down past the ford into deep water. It was curious to watch the behavior of the mules in these teams. As the water rose over their backs they began rearing and springing vertically upward, and as they went deep and deeper the less would be seen of them before they made the spring which would bring their bodies half out of the water; then nothing would be seen but their ears above the

water, until by a violent effort the poor brutes would spring
aloft; and indeed after the waters had closed over them, occasionally one would appear in one last plunge high above the
surface.

A Confederate:

On reaching the upper end of the town we could see a long line
of men wading in the Potomac river. It was just break of day
and it was terrible to see the men in the big river with only their
heads above the water . . . the Potomac was rising rapidly.

Longstreet:

The natural difficulties in making such movements were increased by the darkness of the night, a heavy rainstorm flooding
the road with mud and water, and finally by one of our wagons
loaded with wounded running off the bridge, breaking it down
and throwing it headlong into the water. . . . The rear of my
column passed the bridge at 9 o'clock in the morning.

. . . The army on the 13th of July, passed over very quietly—
the bridges having been covered with bushes to prevent the
rumbling of the wheels.

As the last ones crossed the bridge they cut the cable that held
it. . . .

QUARTERMASTER-GENERAL'S OFFICE,
*Washington, July 20, 1863*
General D. H. Rucker,
*Chief Quartermaster, U.S. Army, Washington:*
GENERAL: It is proposed, as I am informed, by the General-in-Chief to establish a depot for prisoners of war at Point Lookout. . . .
Old tents should be sent from those in depot and necessary camp and garrison equipage, lumber to erect kitchens and storehouses, and large cast-iron boilers for cooking. The labor will be performed by the prisoners themselves.

John R. King:

The 20th of May 1864, we marched through the big gate marked in large letters, "Prisoner's Camp." Now our campaigns were ended. . . . The prison at Point Lookout was located on a narrow piece of ground about one quarter of a mile wide at the mouth of the Potomac River. Here the river is ten miles in width.

Anthony M. Keiley:

The military prison, or rather prisons, at Point Lookout, consisted of two inclosures, the one containing about thirty, the other about ten acres of flat sand, on the northern shore of the Potomac at its mouth, but a few inches above high tide, and utterly innocent of trees, shrub, or any natural equivalent.

THE DIARY OF BARTLETT YANCEY MALONE

Bartlett Y. Malone was borned and raised in North Carolina Caswell County in the Year of our Lord 1838. And was Gradguated in the corn field and tobacco patch: And inlisted in the war June the 18th 1861. And was a member of the Caswell Boys Company. . . .

His purposes will ripen fast
Unfolding evry hour
The bud may have a bitter taste
But sweet will be the flower

May your days be days of pleasure
May your nites be nites of rest
May you obtain lifes sweetest pleasure
And then be numbered with the blest.

———————

Whar ere you rome
What ere your lot
Its all I ask
Forget me not.

Remember me when I am gon
Dear friend remember me
And when you bow befour the throne
O then remember me.

———————

Candy is sweet
It is very clear
But not half so sweet
As you my dear

———————

One day amidst the plas
Where Jesus is within
Is better than ten thousen days
Of pleasure and of Sin

O for grace our hearts to soften
Teach us Lord at length to love

We alas forget too often
What a friend we have above.

All I like of being a Whale
Is a water Spout and a tail.

———————

A certain cewer for the Toothack if the the tooth is hollow
take a pease of the scale that is on a horses leg and put it in the
hollow of the tooth    It is a serten cewer so sais J. H. Lyon.

                                                      B. Y. M.

THIS IS FOR THE YEAR 1863

. . . We was then cutoff and had to Surender: was then taken back
to the rear and stiad thir untell next morning    The morning of
the 8th we was marched back to Warrenton Junction and got on
the cars about day next morning we got to Washington we then
staid in Washington untel 3 o'clock in the eavning of the 8th then
was marched down to the Warf and put on the Stemer John
Brooks and got to Point Lookout about one O'clock on the
eavning of the 10th day of November 1863. . . .

Our rations at Point Lookout was 5 crackers and a cup of
coffee for Breakfast. And for dinner a small ration of meat 2
crackers three Potatoes and a cup of Soup. Supper we have non.
We pay a dollar for 8 crackers or a chew of tobacco for a cracker.

A Yankey shot one of our men the other day wounded him in
the head shot him for peepen threw the cracks of the plan-
ken. . . .

The 24th day of Dec. 63 was a clear day but very cool. And
Generl Butler the Yankey beast revewed the prisners camp:

The 25th was Christmas day and it was clear and cool and I
was both coal and hungry all day only got a peace of Bread and a
cup of coffee for Breakfast and a small Slice of Meat and a cup of
Soup and five Crackers for Dinner and Supper I had non:

The 26th was clear and cool and dull for Christmas.

The 28th was cloudy and rained a littel    The 28th was a raney
day.

The 29th was cloudy in the morning and clear in the eavning.
And Jeferson Walker died in the morning    he belonged to the
57th N. C. Regt. The 30th was a beautyful day.

The 31st which was the last day of 63 was a raney day. And
maby I will never live to see the last day of 64. And thairfour I

will try to do better than I have. For what is a man profited if he
shal gain the whole world and loose his one Soul: Or what Shal
one give in exchange for his Soul:

B. Y. MALONE

B. Y. MALONE'S BOOK
FOR THE YEAR 1864

I spent the first day of January 64 at Point Lookout M. D. The
morning was pleasant but toward eavning the air changed and
the nite was very coal.    was so coal that five of our men froze to
death befour morning. We all suffered a great deal with coal and
hunger too of our men was so hungry to day that they caught a
Rat and cooked him and eat it. Thir names was Sergt. N. W.
Hester & I. C. Covington.

The 6th was coal and cloudy and we had 9 men to die at the
Hospital to day. Our beds at this plaice is composed of Sea
feathers that is we geather the small stones from the Bay and lye
on them

The 7th was very cool a small Snow fell after nite

The 10 was a nice day and I saw the man to day that makes
Coffens at this plaice for the Rebels and he sais that 12 men dies
here every day that is averidgs 12

The Commander at this point is named Marsto

The 22th day of January 64 was a very pritty day And it was
my birth day which maid me 25 years of age    I spent the day at
Point Lookout. M. D. And I feasted on Crackers and Coffee.
The two last weeks of January was beautyfull weather. . . .

The 18th it was so coal that a mans breath would freeze on his
beard going from the Tent to the Cookhouse. O, it was so coal
the 18th.

King:

Two days out of every three we were guarded by a gang of
ignorant and cruelsome negroes.

Please do not think that I dislike the negroes. . . . The negro
guard was very insolent and delighted in tantalizing the prisoners for some trifle affair. . . . "Look out, white man, the
bottom rail is on top now."

Shotwell:

The lower portion of the Pen was occupied by rows of small tents or pretense of tents, they being a lot of condemned canvas, ruined by salt water and mildewed.
. . . From seven to ten men were huddled in each tent like a sweltering nest of pigs.

In rainy weather the rotten canvas served to gather and pour down upon us steady streams of water . . . while within an hour after the rain ceased, great clouds of dry sand began their tireless whirling.

Keiley:

During the scorching summer, whose severity during the day is as great on that sand-barren as anywhere in the Union north of the Gulf, and through the hard winter, which is more severe at that point than anywhere in the country south of Boston, these poor fellows were confined here in open tents, on the naked ground, without a plank or a handful of straw between them and the heat or frost of the earth.

And when, in the winter, a high tide and an easterly gale would flood the whole surface of the pen, *and freeze as it flooded,* the sufferings of the half-clad wretches . . . may easily be imagined. . . .

During all this season the ration of wood allowed to each man was an arm-full for five days, and this had to cook for him as well as warm him, for at the time there were no public cook-houses and mess-rooms.

I never saw any one get enough of any thing to eat at Point Lookout, except the soup, and a teaspoonful of that was *too much* for ordinary digestion.

These digestive discomforts were greatly enhanced by the villainous character of the water, which is so impregnated with some mineral as to offend every nose, and induce diarrhoea in almost every alimentary canal. It colors every thing black in which it is allowed to rest, and a scum rises on the top of a vessel, if it is left standing during the night.

Shotwell:

The soup was always luke-warm, and garnished with white worms half an inch long; while the food was gritty with sand and dirt.

Our rations grow daily worse—the soup more watery, the pork fatter and more rancid, the beef leaner and more stringy.

The camp was full of haggard, half-clad men, whose sunken eyes, and tottering gait bespoke them already doomed. . . .

Washington, *November 13, 1863*
Dr. J. H. DOUGLAS
*Associate Secretary, Sanitary Commission:*
SIR: In compliance with orders received from the central office to proceed to Point Lookout, Md., and inquire into the condition, &c., of the rebel prisoners there confined, also the sanitary condition of the encampment and its inmates, I hereby submit the following report:
. . . No attention was given to the separating of different diseases. Wounded and erysipelas, fever and diarrhea, were lying side by side. . . . There being no stoves in the hospital, the men complained greatly of cold, and I must admit that for the poor emaciated creatures suffering from diarrhea, one single blanket is not sufficient. . . .
The grounds around the hospital have not, according to looks, been policed for a very long time. Filth is gradually accumulating and the sinks are not at all thought of, requiring a little extra exertion to walk to them. They void their excrement in the most convenient place to them, regardless of the comfort of others. . . .
They are ragged and dirty and very thinly clad. . . . Some are without shirts, or what were once shirts are now hanging in shreds from their shoulders. . . . Generally they have one blan-

ket to three men, but a great many are entirely without. . . . A
great many of the tents have been pitched over old sinks lightly
covered. . . . They are troubled greatly with the itch. . . .

Very respectfully, your obedient servant,

W. F. SWALM.

King:

Bathing in the bay was a source of pleasure granted us . . . it was
a great relief to stand on the beach and watch the ships and small
craft pass . . . some with a line and net waded in the water waist
deep and caught the big crabs. . . . When the tide was coming
in the water was delightful, at the dead line we sat on the post
until the waves were highest, then we rode them to the shore.

Right or wrong, God judge me, not man. For be my motive good or bad, of one thing I am sure, the lasting condemnation of the North. I love peace more than life. Have loved the Union beyond expression. For four years have I waited, hoped and prayed for the dark clouds to break and for a restoration of our former sunshine. To wait longer would be a crime. All hope for peace is dead. My prayers have proved as idle as my hopes. God's will be done. I go to see and share the bitter end.

I have ever held the South were right. The very nomination of Abraham Lincoln, four years ago, spoke plainly war, war, upon southern rights and institutions. His election proved it. "Await an overt act." Yes, till you are bound and plundered. What folly. The South was wise. Who thinks of argument or pastime when the finger of his enemy presses the trigger?

The country was formed for the white, not for the black man. And looking upon *African slavery* from the same standpoint held by the noble framers of our constitution, I, for one, have ever considered it one of the greatest blessings (both for themselves and us) that God ever bestowed upon a favored nation. Witness heretofore our wealth and power; witness their elevation and enlightenment above their race elsewhere. I have lived among it most of my life, and have seen *less* harsh treatment from master to man than I ever beheld in the North from father to son. . . .

When I aided in the capture and execution of John Brown (who was a murderer on our Western border and who was fairly tried and convicted, before an impartial judge and jury, of treason, and who, by the way, has since been made a god) I was proud of my little share in the transaction, for I deemed it my duty that I has helping our common country to perform an act of justice. But what was a crime in poor John Brown is now considered (by themselves) as the greatest and only virtue of the whole Republican party. Strange transmigration. *Vice* so becomes a *virtue,* simply because more indulged in. . . .

Alas, poor country. Is she to meet her threatened doom? Four years ago I would have given a thousand lives to see her remain (as I had always known her) powerful and unbroken. And even now I would hold my life as naught to see her what she was. O, my friends, if the fearful scenes of the past four years had never been enacted, or if what has been was a frightful dream, from which we could now awake, with what overflowing hearts could we bless our God. . . .

My love, (as things stand to-day) is for the South alone. Nor do I deem it a dishonour in attempting to make for her a prisoner of this man to whom she owes so much misery. If success attends me, I go penniless to her side. They say she has found that "last ditch" which the North has so long derided, and been endeavoring to force her in, forgetting they are our brothers, and that it is impolitic to goad an enemy to madness. . . .
A confederate doing duty upon his own responsibility.

J. WILKES BOOTH.

FORD'S THEATRE

*Tenth Street, above E*

Friday Evening, April 14th, 1865

*This Evening*
*the Performance will be honored*
*by the presence of*
PRESIDENT LINCOLN

BENEFIT AND LAST NIGHT OF
*Miss* LAURA KEENE
in
Tom Taylor's Celebrated Eccentric Comedy,
as originally produced in America by Miss Keene,
and performed by her upwards of
one thousand nights,
entitled

OUR AMERICAN COUSIN

General and Mrs. Ulysses S. Grant planned to attend the performance with the president's party, but at the last moment the Grants
withdrew (Mrs. Grant couldn't stand Mrs. Lincoln), and the president invited instead Major Henry R. Rathbone and his fiancée, Miss
Clara Harris.

The performance began at 7:45, but the presidential party didn't
appear until 8:30. As Lincoln entered his box, the players halted, the
orchestra struck up "Hail to the Chief," and the audience rose, waved
handkerchiefs, and cheered. Lincoln bowed, then took his seat and
the play resumed.

The president was to be guarded by John F. Parker, special guard, but he and Lincoln's coachman went out for a drink, and when Parker came back he took a seat in the dress circle, so he could see the show.

During the second act, John Wilkes Booth appeared in the alley to the stage door, leading a bay mare. Ordering a stage hand to hold the mare, he entered the theater, passed under the stage to the front of the building, came out on the street, and dropped into the nearest tavern for a drink (he had been drinking heavily recently—a quart of brandy downed in two hours was not unusual).

Later, he emerged. The third act was now playing. He entered the lobby. Passing the doorkeeper, he climbed the stairs to the dress circle and worked his way around the wall to the rear of the private boxes.

Presenting a card to Lincoln's footman, he brushed past him, entered the presidential box, closed the door and barred it from within.

-------

Mary Lincoln laughed. Instantly there was a sound like the report of a firearm, muffled but distinct. Hawk [the actor on stage] thought it came from the property room. Then at the front of the President's box he saw a man brandishing a knife.

Shouting words that Hawk did not understand, the man was over the balustrade. He landed upon the stage in a kneeling posture, about two feet out from the lower box next to the footlights, making a long rent in the green-baize stage carpet. . . . Buckingham, the doorkeeper, . . . got sight of the man crossing toward the "prompt side"—crossing rapidly, with a gait that Mrs. Wright described as "like the hopping of a bull-frog," flourishing the knife as he went.

. . . Smoke drifted out of the President's box. For a moment the greater part of the audience sat as if in a trance.

Abruptly, from within the box, a piercing scream rang out—and the house became an inferno.

There will never be anything like it on earth. The shouts, groans, curses, smashing of seats, screams of women, shuffling of feet and cries of terror created a pandemonium.

There were shouts of "Hang him!" "Kill him!" Chairs were torn from their fastenings. Many persons were in tears. Actors and actresses were jumbled in confusion on the stage with those of the audience who kept mounting it. Some of the musicians had left their instruments behind them. Mrs. Wright put her foot through a 'cello that she seems to have been trying to use as a ladder.

I had never witnesesed such a scene as was now presented. The seats, aisles, galleries, and stage were filled with shouting, frenzied men and women, many running aimlessly over one another; a chaos of disorder beyond control.

Outside, a crowd gathered in the street, shouting "Burn the theater!"

_____

Emerging in the alley, Booth knocked down the man holding his horse, mounted and spurred the mare, rode up the alley to F Street, and was seen to turn right.

_____

The ball entered the skull about midway between the left ear and the median line of the back of the head. . . .

Lincoln tried to rise, lifting his head, "and then it hung back."

Some called for water, others for brandy and a surgeon. A navy doctor, in uniform, clambered onto the stage, was lifted into the box. A pitcher of water was handed up to him.

Major Rathbone, slashed in the arm, dislodged the bar across the door, at the back of the box.

The president, still breathing, was lifted from his chair, carried down the stairs from the dress circle, across the street, and into the Petersen House, a private home.

Laura Keene, standing in the lobby, by the ticket window, exclaimed, in full theatrical voice: "For God's sake, try to capture the murderer!"

---

Sergeant Silas T. Cobb, on duty at the Washington end of the Navy Yard bridge, across the Anacostia, challenged a rider:

> "Who are you, sir?"
> "My name is Booth."
> "Where are you from?"
> "The city."
> "Where are you going?"
> "I'm going home."
> "And where is your home?"
> "In Charles."
> "What town?"
> "I don't live in any town."
> "Oh, you must live in some town."
> "No, I live close to Beantown but not *in* the town."
> "Why are you out so late? Don't you know you're not allowed to pass after nine o'clock?"
> "That's news to me. I had business in the city and thought if I waited I'd have the moon to ride home by."

Sgt. Cobb passed him.

---

In the Petersen house, after midnight: "In rare moments of silence the President's labored breathing sounded through the hall, rising and falling."

---

Across the Anacostia, Booth took the old T.B. Road, by Silver Hill. He was joined on the way by Davey Herold, co-conspirator. Together, they arrived at Lloyd's barroom in the Surratt House at Surrattsville—now Clinton—around midnight. Booth did not dismount; his leg was swollen and painful. He had broken it, when his spur caught in the draped flag, as he leaped from the box to the stage.

Herold dismounted, roused the sodden Lloyd, brought Booth a drink of whiskey, and a carbine Booth had arranged to pick up (the murder weapon, a derringer, had been dropped at the theater).

The pain in Booth's leg, aggravated by riding, became unbearable. Leaving Surrattsville, he turned away from the Potomac and the boat awaiting him at Port Tobacco, rode through the village of T.B., across Mattawoman Swamp, to the home of Dr. Samuel Mudd, near Bryantown.

Dr. Mudd:

> I was aroused by the noise, and as it was such an unusual thing for persons to knock so loudly, I took the precaution of asking who were there before opening the door. After they had knocked twice more, I opened the door, but before doing so they told me they were two strangers on their way to Washington, that one of their horses had fallen, by which one of the men had broken his leg. On opening the door, I found two men, one on a horse led by the other man who had tied his horse to a tree near by. I aided the man in getting off his horse and into the house, and laid him on a sofa in my parlor.
>
> After getting a light, I assisted him in getting up-stairs where there were two beds, one of which he took. . . .

On examination I found there was a straight fracture of the tibia about two inches above the ankle.

The boot was slit across the instep and removed, and the doctor made a splint by doubling a piece of an old bandbox.

It was now daylight.

---

At the Petersen house in Washington, "the measured breathing grew slowly fainter and the sound of it ended." April 15, 7:22 A.M.

---

During the day, Dr. Mudd made the rounds of his patients in Bryantown, while Herold tried unsuccessfully to borrow a carriage in the neighborhood. When Mudd returned in late afternoon, Booth and Herold were gone. Booth carried with him a rough crutch, made for him by a freedman of the place.

Turning again toward the Potomac, they became lost in Zekiah Swamp, tracking and backtracking through the night, until found by Ozzie Swan, a Negro. Swan carried Booth in his wagon and Herold followed with the horses, to the home of Samuel Cox, land owner and Southern sympathizer, not far from Faulkner. It was, again, daybreak.

Cox hid the men in a dense pine thicket, and sent for his foster brother, one Thomas Jones, official Confederate agent in the area.

Jones:

> I have often observed when there is a weighty matter to be discussed between men, how reluctant they seem to approach it. Cox had a most important disclosure to make to me; I knew that he had, and yet, for some minutes, we spoke of any matter rather than that which had brought us together. At length he said to me: "Tom, I had visitors about four o'clock this morning."
>
> "Who were they, and what did they want?" I asked.
>
> "They want to get across the river," said Cox, answering my last question first; and then added in a whisper, "Have you heard that Lincoln was killed Friday night?"
>
> I said, "Yes, I have heard it," . . . There was silence between us for a minute, which was broken by Cox.
>
> "Tom, we must get those men who were here this morning across the river."

The place where Booth and Herold were in hiding was about two hundred yards south of the present village of Cox Station. . . . As I drew near the hiding place I saw a bay mare, with saddle and bridle on, grazing in a small open space where a clearing had been made for a tobacco bed. I at first thought that she belonged to some one in the neighborhood and had got away. I caught her and tied her to a tree. I then went on a little further until I thought I was near the place indicated by Cox. I stopped and gave the whistle. Presently a young man—he looked scarcely more than a boy—came cautiously out of the thicket and stood before me. He carried a carbine ready cocked in his hands.

"Who are you, and what do you want?" he demanded.

"I come from Cox," I replied; "he told me I would find you here. I am a friend; you have nothing to fear from me."

He looked searchingly at me for a moment and then said, "Follow me," and led the way for about thirty yards into the thick undergrowth to where his companion was lying. "This friend comes from Captain Cox," he said; and that was my introduction to John Wilkes Booth. . . .

I told him that I would do what I could to help him; but for the present he must remain where he was; that it would not do to stir during the hue and cry then being made in the neighborhood. I promised to bring him food every day, and to get him across the river, if possible, just as soon as it would not be suicidal to make the attempt.

He held out his hand and thanked me.

He told me, as he had told Cox, that he had killed President Lincoln. He said he knew the United States Government would use every means in its power to secure his capture. "But," he added, with a flash of determination lighting up his dark eye, "John Wilkes Booth will never be taken alive;" and as I looked at him, I believed him.

He seemed very desirous to know what the world thought of his deed, and asked me to bring him some newspapers.

I mentioned to Booth that I had seen a horse grazing near by, and he said it belonged to him. I told him and Herold that they would have to get rid of their horses or they would certainly betray them; besides, it would be impossible to feed them.

Before leaving, I pointed out to Herold a spring about thirty or forty yards distant, where he could procure water for himself and companion. I advised him to be very cautious in going to the spring, as there was a footpath running near it that was sometimes, though seldom, used. Then promising to see them next day and bring food and newspapers, I mounted my horse and rode home.

———————

Herold led the horses into shallow water, over quicksand, and shot them . . .

———————

Jones:

There were but two boats on this side the river that I knew of, and they were both mine. . . .

It need not be said that Booth's only chance for crossing the river depended upon my being able to retain possession and control of one of these two boats.

When I reached home from my visit to Booth that Sunday, I called Henry Woodland, who had continued to live with me after his emancipation, and told him to get out some gill-nets next morning and to fish them regularly every day, and after fishing always to return the boat to Dent's Meadow.

Dent's Meadow was then a very retired spot back of Huckleberry farm, about one and a half miles north of Pope's Creek, at least a mile from the public road and with no dwelling house in sight. This meadow is a narrow valley opening to the river between high and steep cliffs that were then heavily timbered and covered with an almost impenetrable undergrowth of laurel. A small stream flows through the meadow, widening into a little creek as it approaches the river. It was from this spot I determined to make the attempt of sending Booth across to Virginia.

Immediately after breakfast on Monday morning, I wrapped up some bread and butter and ham, filled a flask with coffee, and put it all in the pockets of my overcoat. I then took a basket of corn on my arm as though I were going to call my hogs that ran at large in the woods surrounding my house, and mounting my horse, set out on my dangerous visit. . . .

Nothing of any especial importance happened at this interview. Booth seemed to be suffering more with his leg than on the previous day, and was impatient to resume his journey so as to reach some place where he could be housed and get medical attention. I told him he must wait. While we were talking I heard the clanking of sabers and tramping of horses, as a body of cavalry passed down the road within two hundred yards of us. We listened with suspended breath until the sound died away in the distance. I then said, "You see, my friend, we must wait."

Tuesday morning, after my visit to the pine thicket, I rode up to Port Tobacco.

Tuesday was then, as it is now, the day for the transaction of public business in our county. I was therefore likely to meet a good many people in the county-town that day, and hear whatever was going on.

I found the men gathered about in little groups on the square. . . . The general impression seemed to be that Booth had not crossed the river.

I mingled with the people and listened till I was satisfied that nothing was positively known. Every expression was merely surmise.

Wednesday and Thursday passed uneventfully away. The neighborhood was filled with cavalrymen and detectives. They visited my house several times during that week (as they did every house in southern Maryland) and upon one occasion searched it. They also interviewed my colored man, Henry Woodland, and threatened him with dire penalties if he did not tell all he knew. Henry did not *know* anything because I had told him nothing. I took no one into my confidence. . . .

As the days rolled away, Booth's impatience to cross the river became almost insufferable. His leg, from neglect and exposure, had become terribly swollen and inflamed, and the pain he had to bear was excruciating. To add to his further discomfiture— if that was possible—a cold, cloudy, damp spell of weather, such as we often have in spring, set in and continued throughout the week. . . . The only breaks in the monotony of that week were my daily visits, and the food and newspapers I carried him. He never tired of the newspapers.

Booth—from fragments of a diary:

*April 13–14    Friday the Ides*
I struck boldly and not as the paper say. I walked with a firm step through a thousand of his friends, was stopped but pushed on. A colonel was at his side. I shouted Sic semper *before* I fired. In jumping broke my leg. I passed all his pickets, rode sixty miles that night with the bone of my leg tearing the flesh at every jump. I can never repent it, though we hated to kill. Our country owed all her troubles to him, and God simply made me the instrument of his punishment. The country is not what it *was*. This forced union is not what I have loved. I care not what becomes of me.

Jones:

On Friday evening, one week after the assassination, I rode down to Allen's Fresh. . . .
Allen's Fresh, about three miles east of my house, was and still is, a small village situated where Zechiah Swamp ends and the Wicomico River begins.
I had not been long in the village when a body of cavalry, guided by a man from St. Mary's County named John R. Walton, rode in and dismounted. Some of the soldiers entered Colton's store, where I was sitting, and called for something to drink. Soon afterward Walton came in and exclaimed, "Boys, I have news that they have been seen in St. Mary's," whereupon

they all hastily remounted their horses and galloped off across the bridge in the direction of St. Mary's County.

I was confident there were no other soldiers in the neighborhood.

"Now or never," I thought. . . .

It was dark by the time I reached the place. I had never before visited the fugitives at night: I therefore approached with more than usual caution and gave the signal. Herold answered and led the way to Booth. I informed them of what had just occurred at Allen's Fresh.

"The coast seems to be clear," I said, "and the darkness favors us. Let us make the attempt.". . .

With difficulty Booth was raised by Herold and myself and placed upon my horse. Every movement, in spite of his stoicism, wrung a groan of anguish from his lips. His arms were then given to him, the blankets rolled up and tied behind him on the horse, and we began the perilous journey.

The route we had to take was down the cart track . . . to the public road, a distance of about one mile and a half, then down the public road for another mile to the corner of my farm; and then through my place to the river, about one mile further.

. . . After what seemed an interminable age, we reached my place. We stopped under a pear tree near the stable, about forty or fifty yards from my house. It was then between nine and ten o'clock. "Wait here," I said, "while I go in and get you some supper, which you can eat here while I get something for myself.". . .

I entered the house through the kitchen. Henry Woodland was there. He had got in late and was just eating his supper. I asked him how many shad he had caught that evening and he told me. I then said, "Did you bring the boat to Dent's Meadow, and leave it there, Henry?"

"Yes, master."

"We had better get out another net to-morrow," I replied. "The fish are running well."

Some members of my family were in the dining-room when I entered. My supper was on the table waiting for me. I selected what I thought was enough for the two men and carried it out to them. None of the family seemed to notice what I was doing. They knew better than to question me about anything in those days.

After supper we resumed our journey across the open field toward the longed-for river. . . . Presently we came to a fence that ran across the path, about three hundred yards from the river. It was difficult to take it down; so we left the horse there and Herold and myself assisted Booth to dismount and supporting him between us, took our way carefully down the tortuous path that led to the shore.

The path was steep and narrow and for three men to walk down it abreast, one of them being a cripple, to whom every step was torture, was not the least difficult part of that night's work.

But the Potomac, that longed-for goal, at last was near.

It was nearly calm now, but the wind had been blowing during the day and there was a swell upon the river, and as we approached, we could hear its sullen roar. It was a mournful sound coming through the darkness. . . .

At length we reached the shore and found the boat where Henry had been directed by me to leave it. It was a flat bottomed boat about twelve feet long, of a dark lead color. . . .

We placed Booth in the stern with an oar to steer; Herold took the bow-seat to row. Then lighting a candle which I had brought for the purpose—I had no lantern—and carefully shading it with an oilcloth coat belonging to one of the men, I pointed out on the compass Booth had with him the course to steer. "Keep to that," I said, "and it will bring you into Machodoc Creek. Mrs. Quesenberry lives near the mouth of this creek. If you tell her you come from me I think she will take care of you." . . .

I pushed the boat off and it glided out of sight into the darkness.

I stood on the shore and listened till the sound of the oars died away in the distance.

---

Jones failed or forgot to warn them of the spring flood tide. The boat was carried upstream, along the Maryland shore, and Herold finally put into Avon Creek, a tributary of Nanjemoy. Throughout the day Saturday, he and Booth remained in concealment.

Booth's diary:

> After being hunted like a dog through swamps, woods, and last night being chased by gun-boats till I was forced to return wet cold and starving, with every man's hand against me, I am here in despair. And why? For doing what Brutus was honored for. What made Tell a hero. And yet I for striking down a greater tyrant than ever they knew am looked upon as a common cutthroat. My action was purer than either of theirs. . . . I hoped for no gain. I knew no private wrong. I struck for my country and that alone. A country groaned beneath this tyranny and prayed for this end, and yet now behold the cold hand they extend to me. . . . So ends all. For my country I have given up all that makes life sweet and Holy, brought misery upon my family, and am sure there is no pardon in the Heaven for me since man condemn me so. . . . To night I will once more try the river with the intent to cross. . . .
>
> I have too great a soul to die like a criminal. Oh may he, may he spare me that and let me die bravely.

———————

Saturday night, Booth and Herold crossed the Potomac, landing in Gambo Creek, just above Machadoc. Helped by Mrs. Quesenberry and others, they made their way inland to the Rappahannock, ferried across at Port Royal, and rode three miles further, along the Bowling Green road, to the Garrett farm, where they were taken in, fed, and housed, passing as Confederate veterans.

Booth spent the day—Tuesday, April 25th—reclining on the front porch, with a view of rolling hills and a stretch of the approaching road.

That night, he and Herold, becoming suspicious, moved out of the house to the tobacco barn. The Garrett boys sat up to watch them, thinking they might be horse thieves.

———————

Two o'clock Wednesday morning, the Garrett yard was suddenly filled with Union cavalry. The elder Garrett was awakened and questioned, but would not say where the fugitives were. When the soldiers threatened to hang him, his son, Jack Garrett, directed them to the tobacco barn.

Surrounding the barn, the officers parleyed with Booth, who refused to surrender. Young Garrett was sent in to disarm the men, but quickly emerged, terrorized.

At length, Herold: "Let me out! Let me out!"
The door opened, and he was passed out to the soldiers, unarmed and shaking.

Igniting loose hay from a candle, the soldiers set fire to the barn; spreading to hay inside, the flames quickly took off, and Booth, armed at both hands and leaning on crutches, appeared in silhouette through the open slats. He dropped one crutch, then the other, and with "a kind of limping, halting jump," moved toward the door. A shot rang out, Booth sprang forward, and fell in a heap.

He was dragged, still living, from the burning barn, and carried to the porch of the farmhouse.
"Kill me! Kill me!" he whispered . . . One of the Garrett women brought him a pillow, but he could not be made comfortable.

. . . Between five and six—at daybreak—his breathing stopped.

---

Booth had been shot by Boston Corbett, one of the soldiers.
"Why in hell did you shoot without orders?" his officer asked.
Corbett came to attention, and saluted. "Colonel, Providence directed me."

# Part Three

# Nineteen Sixties

ONE

My pedestrian excursions of the last year had given me a relish for these rambles; I had become convinced that they were both easy, usefull and full of pleasure, while they afforded me the means to study every thing at leasure. I never was happier than when alone in the woods.

. . .Constantine Samuel Rafinesque, naturalist, exploring the Potomac region, 1804-1805. (His real name was not Constantine Samuel Rafinesque, but Constantine Samuel Rafinesque Schmaltz.)

I collected many rare and new plants at the falls of Potowmack. I went to Alexandria to visit the herbal of Hingston, who gave me several rare plants. The heat becoming oppressive I returned.

. . . Next to Frederic by the rail road. There I took the Washington stage to reach the foot of the Sugarloaf, a singular insulated mt. 15 miles around and 500 feet high, (Long says 800), it is primitive, an avant post of the Cotocton mts. yet omitted in nearly all the maps. I herborized there and went afterwards to the Point of rocks or lower water gap of R. Potomak, in the Cotocton mts.

Crossing the river here into Virginia, I began my pedestrian rambles; but had to contend against muddy roads and repeated showers. . . . I took Harper's ferry stage for 15 miles to be left in the mts.; thus surveying them well, and botanizing in the mts., the banks of the Potowmak and Shenandoah rivers.

In the South Branch area today, a big-eared bat, first identified by Rafinesque, may be found.

## TWO

The jagged granitic hills, Precambrian, in what is now the Potomac area, were wind- and rainswept, relieved only by scattered, primitive algal growths.

Cracks opened in the earth's crust, long fissures, and layer upon layer of molten lava poured out,

       hardened,

           and metamorphosed into

greenstone . . .

Weighted and eroded, the land sank, and waters from the Atlantic and Gulf seeped in to form an inland sea—the Paleozoic Sea— the major surfacing land mass lying to the east.

The sea filled a long, narrow trough from the Canadian Shield through the Virginia Piedmont and southward, the waters shifting, ebbing and flowing, land-locked and ocean-connected, fresh and marine, but always shallow, with low, sandy or muddy banks, scattered islands, low capes and peninsulas, straits, lagoons, and inlets.

Mud, sand, and gravel washed into the trough from the eastward land masses, at a rate equaling that of subsidence, and the sea remained evenly shallow. Great lenticular layers of sediments were formed—shale, sandstone, and conglomerate, with limy muds, and shell fragments of coral, clam, snail, and crab-like animals—brachiopods, trilobites, and gastropods—to form limestone.

In Devonian time, overgrown ferns and club mosses appeared. There were fish, similar to shark and sturgeon, and, on land, giant salamanders. Later, in Mississippian, the ferns, club mosses, and horsetails grew gigantically, decayed furiously, to form coal.

Toward the end of the Paleozoic era, subsidence of the trough ceased and the Appalachian Revolution began: unknown forces (resulting, perhaps, from continental drift) thrust the earth's crust upward, the Paleozoic Sea fled to the west, and there was great horizontal movement, exerting lateral pressure, southeast to northwest. Earthquakes were common, and the granites, lavas, and sea-floor sediments were wrinkled, folded, shoved, and fractured. Anticline arches broke, elongate blocks were overthrust northwestward, over underlying rocks. Sandstone cliffs stood on end:

The Mother Appalachians grew into being, upwarping, higher and more rugged than the present hills.

Attacked at once by weather and streams, the slopes eroded, spreading muds, sands, and limy silts eastward into down-warped basins, over the Piedmont, and into tidal estuaries . . . until the region was worn to a vast and gently rolling plain, a peneplain in which only truncated mountain roots remain.

The ocean level rose and fell, successively sedimenting Tidewater, the Piedmont-Tidewater border (the fall line) being a shifting shoreline.

Once again, accumulated internal forces came into action: the peneplain uplifted and the broad, sluggish streams, meandering at leisure over the flat terrain, became rejuvenated. Cutting into their beds, flowing faster and more steeply, carrying more sediment, the rivers stripped the softer shales and limestones, leaving the more durable ridges of modern Appalachia.

The east-flowing streams—having a steeper gradient and being closer to their base-level, the ocean—carved back into the headwater divides, pirating the west-flowing stream heads, flowing eastward through Valley and Ridge Province, and—sawing through hard rock and ridge—opening a way to the Atlantic.

At Harper's Ferry, the Potomac once flowed across a plain higher than the tops of the present mountains. As the land rose, the river cut its way down and through, leaving terraces in hard and soft rock alike.

Less powerful streams followed their valleys, seeking a natural outlet, producing on the corrugated landscape a trellis effect.

The Shenandoah, young and sporadic, began at Harper's Ferry and carved its way up the Valley, capturing established streams right and left, converting water gaps into wind gaps, beheading the Rappahannock, the Rapidan, the Rivanna.

The Shenandoah in the Seven Bends and the Potomac at Paw Paw Bends preserve their original peneplain meanders, now incised in the uplifted land.

---

Dinosaurs, pterosaurs, and other gigantic reptiles thrived during the Mesozoic era. Fossil leaves, lignitized tree trunks, occasional dinosaur bones are found in Potomac formations. The remains of a cypress swamp were uncovered in excavations in Washington.

Modern vegetation came into being during the last 15 to 20 million years.

---

Today the upper Potomac harbors relict plants from glacial vegetation. Ice never entered West Virginia, but the region serves as a refuge for northern plants: the paper birch is found here, and the red pine reaches its southernmost points of unassisted growth, on South Branch and North Fork Mountains.

On Spruce Mountain and along the Allegheny Front nesting sites are found for the golden-crowned kinglet, the winter wren, Swainson's thrush, magnolia warbler, and purple finch—species characteristic of the spruce forests of Canada. At lower elevations are the characteristically southern black vulture and loggerhead shrike. During June and July, on shaly grounds, the yellow blossoms of the prickly pear cactus appear, reminiscent of western deserts. In September, the rains of Atlantic hurricanes blow in from the east.

Endemic to the shale barrens are the bindweed, the whitehaired leatherflower, the shale ragwort, shale primrose, shale goldenrod . . . the knotweed . . .

The golden eagle used to nest at Potomac headwaters, was exterminated during the 1930s and '40s, as a varmint. He may occasionally be seen from North Fork Mountain or Hawk Mountain, in migration.

At Reddish Knob, the raven and the red-tailed hawk
  a great horned owl on Thorn Creek
  crossbills, siskins, and grosbeaks
  a grebe at Upper Tract
  a loon from the north, a chat from the south . . .

       the red-headed woodpecker . . .

------

In the Smoke Hole, on the South Branch, there is bear sign and shadblow . . .
  mosses and lichens, white ceder, Virginia pine
  columbine, polypody fern, lovegrass and bent grass, maidenhair and hairy lip fern, the purple cliffbrake
  in the depths of the Hole, the crested coralroot, a southern orchid here reaching its northern limit.

Up from the Hole, on the Tuscarora sandstone along the crest of North Fork Mountain, and other sandstone ridges, the silvery whitlow-wort, growing here and nowhere else . . .

------

To be found in Shenandoah National Park are ninebark, bull thistle, oldfield cinquefoil . . .
  fourleaf loosestrife, nodding onion, glorybird

---

On the ground: the black racer and the blue-tailed skink.

In the water, five cats: channel, yellow, bullhead, Potomac, madtom.
  Also, large-mouth black bass, crappie and calico bass, rock bass in Rock Run . . .

On Sugarloaf Mountain there is table mountain pine, and acres of milkvetch on Massanutten
  wineleaf cinquefoil on North Fork Mountain
  nailworts and quill flameflower at Seneca Rocks . . . at Dolly Sods, red spruce . . .

In 1915, sunfish were abundant in ponds on the rocky headland just below Difficult Run. Other fish taken in Potomac waters were the sea lamprey, the fork-tailed and red-eyed cats, chub sucker and horned chub, black-nosed dace and goggle-eye.

Sunfish, cats, and black bass ran into Dead Run.

---

In 1876, the Potomac-Side Naturalists' Club compiled a list of 1,083 plant species, also 91 mosses and 28 Hepaticae, growing "in the District of Columbia and its immediate vicinity."

---

A wartime Washington birdwatcher reported, 1940s, that "a drake American merganser on the Basin was swimming in tight circles about the dead body of a female floating on its side so that only an upturned section of its underparts showed above-water. After two minutes in which the male was obviously invoking the powers of life, he climbed onto the dead body and copulated with it, lifting the limp head in his bill. The mystical act accomplished, the female returned to life and swam off happily with her rescuer."

---

Fresh and estuarine, fluctuant by reason of tide and rain, wind and season, the Wicomoco River rises in the coarse-stemmed marsh, the weak-stemmed marsh of Zekiah Swamp. Catbird, brown thrasher, and eastern phoebe may be found here, at the northern limit of winter range, and there is a great blue heron rookery.

In the swamp, in the past, a steady fresh-water flow nourished the wild rice, and on Cobb's Island, at the rivermouth, needlerush, salt-meadow grass, and saltmarsh cordgrass grow.

There are teal, shoveler, and sora on the river, and Wilson's snipe in Allen's Fresh. The gadwall winters on Cuckold Creek, and in late summer there are peep on the mudflats, perhaps a great black-backed gull.

On Swan Neck, at Issue, the loblolly pine has been lumbered . . .

## THREE

On Christmas Eve 1852, the last spike was driven into the Baltimore and Ohio Railroad Line, connecting Cumberland with Wheeling. This marked the beginning of the end for the C & O Canal and for the adjacent stream, the Potomac River:

The railroad, mills, little industries, mines, municipalities—the very people themselves—turned their backsides to the river,

> . . . and shat into it.

———————————

Fairfax Stone, at Potomac headwaters, stands in a patch of woods surrounded by—and within sight of—abandoned strip coal mines. The stream trickles but a few yards before receiving the first sulphuric acid and yellowy iron hydrate extracted by springs, seeps, and runoff water from denuded coal strata and spoil heaps. Five to ten million tons of acid enter the river annually, from abandoned strips and one-man tunnel mines that pock the hillsides—a rate of production expected to continue for at least a thousand years. At George's Creek, solid wastes enter the river in a pickle brine of acid water . . .

complex wastes from textile industries
suspended materials from food processing plants and liquors pressed from wet grains at breweries
pickle liquors and piggery wastes

greasy wastes from tanneries

wastes—ligneous, resinous, and carbonaceous—from pulp and paper plants

penolic, cresolic, ammoniacal, and tarry wastes from gas and coke plants

greasy, soapy water from laundries, and various complex wastes from chemical and rubber industries

As late as 1946, 75 percent of such wastes were sluiced into the Potomac altogether innocent of treatment.

At a pulp and paper mill in Luke, a portion of the vast, complex wastage is dumped raw, to be added to the effluent of the treatment plant.

Towns and villages along the way dump in raw human sewage: brown lumps, toilet paper, unsanitary napkins, together with the loaded effluent of perfunctory primary plants.

In heavy storms at Cumberland, the combined storm and sanitary sewer systems overflow and it all goes raw to the river.

Opequon Creek is fouled with sewage, Conococheague and Antietam creeks import human manure from Pennsylvania, there are chicken feathers and zinc in the Shenandoah.

———————

In Jefferson's day, the mouth of the Anacostia was one mile wide, and the U.S. Navy, entire, sailed up to Bladensburg.

Today, 2.5 million tons of silt and sediment erode into the Potomac annually, to coat the river bottom, foul municipal filtering operations, cover oyster beds, smother fingerling fish, and rasp the gills of survivors. Lazy farming practices and a shriveled, scrubby timber growth contribute to erosion, but the greatest cause is stripping the soil for construction—roadbuilding, home developments, industrial expansion. More than 25,000 tons per square mile of land thus developed may be washed away, topsoil never to be retrieved.

At public expense, the U.S. Army Corps of Engineers dredges the sludge from the shipping channel and collects construction debris from the water surface.

---

The Potomac River serves as the principal supply of drinking water for the District of Columbia. In recent drought years, nearly the entire stream flow—which included raw sewage from thirty-one upstream communities—has been sucked into metropolitan water intakes.

Sewage effluent from the District receives less than 100 percent treatment. Solid wastes pass directly into the river, join detritus flowing from upstream, and rock gently back and forth before Washington in the rising and falling tides (a piece of solid matter requires more than a hundred days to clear the river).

In heavy storms, the antiquated sanitary and storm sewers of the District and Alexandria overflow, the entire effluent charges directly into the estuary,

and seagulls swarm at the storm sewers . . .

The effluents from sewage treament plants, liquid and less toxic, are a rich and oily broth of nitrates and phosphates, stimulating malodorous scums of algal blooms, starving the waters of oxygen. . . . The river, in advanced eutrophication, is suddenly old.

On a warm summer day, when conditions are right, the upper estuary may be "one vast inspired pool of fertility—the whole surface of the river . . . covered with a thick bright emerald mat."

---

*New York Times* News Service, March 24, 1969:

WASHINGTON—The Potomac River is just about as badly polluted as it was a decade ago, despite an extensive clean-up program, the Federal Water Pollution Control Administration has reported.

In its lower reaches, where the river provides a scenic background for the nation's capital, it is so laden with bacteria as to make swimming or any other recreational contact "hazardous," the agency said.

Much of the raw sewage that used to gush into the river and its immediate tributaries at a rate of billions of gallons a year has been eliminated.

But inadequate sewage treatment facilities, increasing population, and a continuing problem of overflows from sewer lines during storms have left the river's water substantially unimproved.

———————

Black bass in the Shenandoah are slaughtered by zinc . . .
   three million alewives killed in the Anacostia
   rock fish floating by the thousands in the lower estuary
   on the shoreline at Mount Vernon, windrows of dead and stinking
carp and perch . . .

———————

J. F. D. Smyth, 1784:

Every advantage, every elegance, every charm, that bountiful nature can bestow, is heaped with liberality and even profufion on the delightful banks of this moft noble and fuperlatively grand river. All the defirable variety of land and water, woods and lawns, hills and dales, tremendous cliffs and lovely vallies, wild romantic precipices and fweet meandering ftreams adorned with rich and delightful meàdows, in fhort all the elegance, beauty, and grandeur that can be conceived in perfpective, are here united, to feaft the fight and foul of thofe who are capable of enjoying the luxurious and fumptuous banquet.

There are seventeen military installations in the metropolitan Washington area, within ten miles of the estuary. Approximately 54 miles of shoreline, and 100,000 acres of land, are included.

President Lyndon Johnson, at the White House Conference on Natural Beauty, May 1965:

> The river rich in history and memory which flows by our Nation's Capital should serve as a model of scenic and recreation values for the entire country. To meet this objective I am asking the Secretary of the Interior to review the Potomac River Basin development plan now under review by the Chief of Army Engineers, and to work with the affected States and local governments, the District of Columbia, and interested Federal agencies to prepare a program for my consideration.
>
> A program must be devised which will—
>
> (a) Clean up the river and keep it clean, so it can be used for boating, swimming, and fishing;
>
> (b) Protect its natural beauties by the acquisition of scenic easements, zoning, or other measures;
>
> (c) Provide adequate recreational facilities.

The plan of the Corps of Engineers involved construction of an 85-foot dam at Riverbend above Washington, impounding 36,000 acres of water surface, destroying canal and shoreline back almost to Harper's Ferry. It was planned to draw down the water level ten feet during dry weather, exposing that much raw mud bank, to provide the Washington area with sufficient volume of water to flush the District sludge downstream.

A later plan proposes construction of the Bloomington Reservoir on the North Branch, to impound the mine-acid waters for presumed recreation.

SIX

Construction of the John F. Kennedy Center for the Performing Arts
stirred up the soil on the flood plain of the Potomac River.

Nearby, one evening in June, three of us picked lamb's-quarters for
dinner at the edge of a vacant lot, corner of 24th and G, N.W. One of
the locals stopped by and helped us, told us that the lot belonged to a
bank (specialists in green stuff) . . .

## SEVEN

The rise in the value of landed property, in this country, has been progressive, ever since my attention has been turned to the subject (now more than 40 years); but for the last three or four of that period, it has increased beyond all calculation. . . . I do not hesitate to pronounce that, the Lands on the Waters of Potomack will, in a few years, be in greater demand, and in higher estimation than in any other part of the United States.

. . . George Washington, 1796.

The two million inhabitants of metropolitan Washington today are expected, by the year 2100, to increase to six million. By 2166, metropolitan Washington will extend to Harper's Ferry.

From "The Social Aspects of Population Dynamics," J. B. Calhoun:

Wherever animals live they are constantly altering the environment about them. This occurs through such diverse phenomena as release of excreta, alteration of surrounding temperature and humidity, construction of trails and burrows, and the development of habits, all of which may alter the behavior of members of their own or later generations.

As soon as animals begin to condition their environment through the elaboration of relatively permanent artifacts such as trails, nests, burrows, and the like, biological conditioning assumes a more definite cultural aspect. To be sure, such artifacts satisfy primary organic requirements: dens are a place of retreat from enemies or inclement weather; nests are places where the young are safe; trails lead to food or harborage, and food caches serve to make food more accessible. However, beyond such primary functions, dens, nests, trails and the like further serve as a physical mold in which the social matrix takes its form.

From *The Hidden Dimension*, Edward T. Hall:

Western man has set himself apart from nature and, therefore, from the rest of the animal world. He could have continued to ignore the realities of his animal constitution if it had not been for the population explosion. . . . This, together with the implosion into our cities of poverty-stricken people from rural areas, has created a condition which has all the earmarks of population buildup and subsequent crash in the animal world. . . .

Many ethologists have been reluctant to suggest that their findings apply to man, even though crowded, overstressed animals are known to suffer from circulatory disorders, heart attacks, and lowered resistance to disease. One of the chief differences between man and animals is that man has domesticated himself by developing his extensions and then proceeding to screen his senses so that he could get more people into a smaller space. Screening helps, but the ultimate buildup can still be lethal. . . .

If one looks at human beings in the way that the early slave traders did, conceiving of their space requirements simply in terms of the limits of the body, one pays very little attention to the effects of crowding. If, however, one sees man surrounded by a series of invisible bubbles which have measurable dimensions, . . . it is then possible to conceive that people can be cramped by the spaces in which they have to live and work. They may even find themselves forced into behavior, relationships, or emotional outlets that are overly stressful. . . . When stress increases, sensitivity to crowding rises—people get more on edge—so that more and more space is required as less and less is available.

Screening is what we get from rooms, apartments, and buildings in cities. Such screening works until several individuals are
crowded into one room; then a drastic change occurs. The walls
no longer shield and protect, but instead press inward on the
inhabitants.

By domesticating himself, man has greatly reduced the flight
distance of his aboriginal state, which is an absolute necessity
when population densities are high. The flight reaction . . . is
one of the most basic and successful ways of coping with danger,
but there must be sufficient space if it is to function. Through a
process of taming, most higher organisms, including man, can
be squeezed into a given area provided that they feel safe and
their aggressions are under control. However, if men are made
fearful of each other, fear resurrects the flight reaction, creating
an explosive need for space. Fear, plus crowding, then produces
panic.

From the *Washington Post*, Saturday, April 6, 1968:

Six thousand armed troops were rushed into Washington's
streets last night and early this morning to combat widespread
burning and looting of the city.

A brigade of paratroopers of the 82nd Airborne Division
from Ft. Bragg, N.C., was to arrive at Andrews Air Force base
shortly after midnight.

At least three are dead from the rioting. . . .

The Mayor imposed a night-long curfew and banned the sale
of liquor and firearms. . . . Brazen looting went on just two
blocks from the White House.

The Pentagon spokesman said at 10 p.m. that at least 950
rioters had been arrested here. . . .

Firemen said there had been at least 170 fires Friday. . . . A
thick pall of smoke hung over the inner city. . . .

The troops, including both regular army and National
Guardsmen, moved into the city with their rifles unloaded but
with ammunition in their belts, their bayonets sheathed.

The troops first cleared H. Street ne., then 14th Street nw.,
two of the worst trouble spots, then moved to side streets. As

they swept along—chanting "March, March, March"—they
would drop off a small contingent to keep control of each
intersection. By 11 p.m., they were stationed in many sections
of the city.

The troops were deployed by means of helicopter. . . .

The disturbance caused cancellation or postponement of a number of events. A spokesman for the Cherry Blossom Festival
announced that all remaining activities of the Festival, including
the annual ball scheduled for last night, have been canceled.

The Washington Senators announced that Monday's open-
ing-day baseball game with the Minnesota Twins had been
rescheduled. . . .

Despite the greater frequency of vandalism and looting, fire
apparently caused the most serious damage.

. . . All evening, police and reporters on the street reported
fires burning with no fire fighting equipment in sight.

. . . Black power advocates at Howard University hauled
down an American flag and raised in its place a flag of their own
design. . . .

When they could, policemen took stolen goods from looters or
barked at them through bullhorns. . . . There was an eerie
holiday mood. . . .

Washington paid an extra price in its day of rioting and looting
yesterday because of a massive traffic jam that tied the city in
knots throughout the afternoon.

Police cars, fire trucks and ambulances were among vehicles
brought to a virtual standstill as an early exodus of downtown
employes clogged all major streets with thousands of autos and
buses.

Adding to the problem was the presence of thousands of
tourists here for the Cherry Blossom Festival. Their slow-
moving cars circulated around the Mall, the Lincoln Memorial
and the Tidal Basin area, blocking commuter routes to the
suburbs.

In their haste, people drove too fast, slipping traffic lights and using their horns. In the street, pedestrians elbowed each other aside in the dash to quit the city.

"Oh God, I'm scared," said a white girl in an elevator in a downtown office building.

A Negro riding at the rear reached over and touched her arm. "Well, I am too," he said.

## EIGHT

The District, Great Falls and Ball's Bluff, Plummer's Island: a zone of floral interdigitation, the species overrunning and intermingling, down and up country, Ridge and Tidewater.

Summersweet clethera, a coastal plant, ascending the Maryland shore, overlapping Appalachian varieties, downstream on the Virginia side.

Potomac and tributary headwaters, scrambling into the Allegheny Front, pirating western springs, became a natural floral highway, importing in flood the seeds of pioneer plants of open or prairie habitat, to become established on expanses of metamorphic granite, schist and gneiss, and in neutral soils on the benches and flood plains, in the interdigital area.

Scrub pine, above the District, is new since Washington's time, moving in where the land has been clear cut, farmed and abandoned, and surviving one generation only, to be replaced by hardwoods.

Sugar maples survive at the mouth of Difficult Run, with a stronger stand at Riverbend.

At Ball's Bluff, the cliffs have never been cut and farmed, and the display is exceptional: dogtooth violet and shooting star . . .

At the Falls, spangle grass and leather-flower, redbud and shadblow . . .

*Notes & Bibliography*

## Imprimis

The interpretations of Indian place names are from the following:

Davis, Julia. *The Shenandoah*. New York, 1945.

Harrison, Fairfax. *Landmarks of Old Prince William*. Richmond, 1924.

Johnston, C. H. L., ed. *The South Branch of the Potomac*. 1931.

Tooker, W. W. "The Algonquin Terms Patawomeke and Massawomeke." *American Anthropologist,* April 1894.

Facts about the size of the Potomac River basin are from the booklet:

University of Maryland, Bureau of Business and Economic Research. *Potomac River Basin*. College Park, 1957.

Place names found on and near the river are taken largely from a study of U.S. Geological Survey maps.

Berkeley Springs, as an Indian gathering place, is described in:

Writers Project, Work Projects Administration. *West Virginia, A Guide to the Mountain State*. New York, 1941.

Description of the Indian fishing villages near Little Falls is from:

Holmes, W. H. *Stone Implements of the Potomac–Chesapeake Tidewater Province*. Washington, 1897.

Indian meanings of place names on the estuary may be found in:

Beitzell, Edwin W. *Life on the Potomac River*. Washington, 1968.

## Discovery and Indians

Material dealing with early Spanish discovery of Chesapeake Bay and the Potomac is taken from:

Lewis, C. M., and Loomie, A. J. *The Spanish Jesuit Mission in Virginia, 1570–1572.* Chapel Hill, 1953.

Regarding identification of the river, which I take to be the Potomac, the authors offer the following in their notes:

It is difficult to say whether the Rappahannock or the Potomac is meant. The latitude is right for the latter, but Gonzales' latitudes are consistently too high. The depth and description of the southern bank applies to both rivers. The valley could be either Urbanna Creek or Yeocomico River. The land on the north bank of the Rappahannock rises to 80 feet, that on the Potomac to 100 feet. . . . Perhaps the strongest argument for the Potomac is the fact that he speaks of the good condition of the land from the 38th degree north, a natural division to make of the western coast line if the Potomac is taken as the starting point.

Discussion of Potomac Indians is derived from the following sources:

Ferguson, A. L. L., and Ferguson, H. G. *The Piscataway Indians of Southern Maryland.* Accokeek, Maryland, 1960.

Graham, William J. *The Indians of Port Tobacco River.* Washington, 1935.

Holmes, W. H. *Stone Implements of the Potomac–Chesapeake Tidewater Province.* Washington, 1897.

Marye, William S. "Piscataway." *Maryland Historical Magazine,* September 1935.

Mason, O. T., ed. *Aborigines of the District of Columbia and Lower Potomac.* Washington, 1889.

Scharf, J. T. *History of Maryland.* Hatboro, Pennsylvania, 1967.

Stephenson, Robert L. *Prehistoric People of Accokeek Creek.* Accokeek, Maryland, 1959.

Writers Project, Work Projects Administration. *Maryland, A Guide to the Old Line State.* New York, 1940.

Accounts of the voyages of John Smith and of Lord Delaware are from the following:

Smith, Bradford. *Captain John Smith.* Philadelphia, 1953.

Tyler, L. G., ed. *Narratives of Early Virginia, 1606–1625.* New York, 1907.

In exploring Chesapeake Bay, Smith apparently sailed northward, along the eastern shore, to a point opposite the Patapsco River and Baltimore harbor, and then crossed to the western shore and coasted southward, until he entered the Potomac.

Material dealing with early Maryland settlement is from:

Hall, C. C., ed. *Narratives of Early Maryland, 1633–1684.* New York, 1910.

## ⟨geography⟩

Facts on the comparative size of the river are taken from:
> Coordinating Committee on the Potomac River Valley. *Potomac Prospect*. Washington, 1961.

## Early Settlement

The first part of this chapter is derived from the following sources:
> Alsop, George. *A character of the province of Maryland*. Cleveland, 1902.
>
> Force, Peter. *Tracts*. Washington, 1836–46.
>
> Hamor, Ralph. *A True Discourse of the Present Estate of Virginia*. 1615.
>
> Harrison, Fairfax. *Landmarks of Old Prince William*. Richmond, 1924.
>
> McAtee, W. L. *A Sketch of the Natural History of the District of Columbia*. Washington, 1918.
>
> Tyler, L. G., ed. *Narratives of Early Virginia, 1606–1625*. New York, 1907.

The quotations from Henry Fleet's journal are taken from:
> Neill, Edward D. *Founders of Maryland*. Albany, 1876.

Instructions for Maryland settlers are found in:
> Hall, C. C., ed. *Narratives of Early Maryland, 1633–1684*. New York, 1910.

The final portions of the chapter are derived from the following:
> Alsop, George. *A character of the province of Maryland*. Cleveland, 1902.
>
> Durand of Dauphiné. *A Huguenot Exile in Virginia*. New York, 1934.
>
> Harrison, Fairfax. *Landmarks of Old Prince William*. Richmond, 1924.
>
> Hart, A. B., ed. *American History Told by Contemporaries*. New York, 1931.
>
> Tyler, L. G., ed. *Narratives of Early Virginia, 1606–1625*. New York, 1907.
>
> U.S. Department of the Interior. *The Nation's River*. Washington, 1968.

## Upriver Exploration

The first two parts of the chapter, on the mountains, are from the following:

Alvord, C., and Bidgood, L. *The First Explorations of the Trans-Allegheny Region by the Virginians, 1650–1674*. Cleveland, 1912.

Durand of Dauphiné. *A Huguenot Exile in Virginia*. New York, 1934.

Force, Peter. *Tracts*. Washington, 1836–46.

Harrison, Fairfax. *Landmarks of Old Prince William*. Richmond, 1924.

Maury, Ann, ed. *Memoirs of a Huguenot Family*. Baltimore, 1967.

Tyler, L. G., ed. *Narratives of Early Virginia, 1606–1625*. New York, 1907.

Following are sources for the section dealing with Indians:

Ambler, C. H. *West Virginia, The Mountain State*. New York, 1940.

Bailey, Kenneth P. *Thomas Cresap, Maryland Frontiersman*. Boston, 1944.

Darlington, W. M., ed. *Christopher Gist's Journals*. Pittsburgh, 1893.

Davis, Julia. *The Shenandoah*. New York, 1945.

Fowke, Gerard. *Archeologic Investigations in James and Potomac Valleys*. Washington, 1894.

Gilbert, Bil. "Exaltation at the Smokehole." *Sports Illustrated*, April 27, 1964.

Harrison, Fairfax. *Landmarks of Old Prince William*. Richmond, 1924.

Johnston, C. H. L., ed. *The South Branch of the Potomac*. 1931.

Marye, W. S. "Patowmeck Above ye Inhabitants." *Maryland Historical Magazine*, March and June, 1935.

Smith, J. Lawrence. *The Potomac Naturalist*. Parsons, West Virginia, 1968.

Material on the two surveys of Potomac headwaters is from the following:

Basset, J. S., ed. *The Writings of Colonel William Byrd*. New York, 1901.

Foster, James W. "Maps of the First Survey of the Potomac River, 1736–1737." *William and Mary Quarterly* 18, nos. 2 and 4.

Kennedy, Philip P. *The Blackwater Chronicle*. New York, 1853.

Lewis, Thomas. *The Fairfax Line; Thomas Lewis's Journal of 1746*. New Market, Virginia, 1925.

Lewis apparently started from Staunton, Virginia; crossed Massanutten Mountain, the Shenandoah Valley, and the South Branch near Petersburg, West Virginia; thence to the North Branch headwaters.

Following are sources for the remainder of this chapter:

Bacon-Foster, Cora. *Early Chapters in the Development of the Potomac Route to the West*. Washington, 1912.

Bailey, Kenneth P. *Thomas Cresap, Maryland Frontiersman*. Boston, 1944.

Browning, Meshach. *Forty-four Years the Life of a Hunter*. Philadelphia, 1859.

Darlington, W. M., ed. *Christopher Gist's Journals*. Pittsburgh, 1893.

Fitzpatrick, John C., ed. *The Diaries of George Washington*. Boston and New York, 1925.

Harrison, Fairfax. *Landmarks of Old Prince William*. Richmond, 1924.

Johnston, C. H. L., ed. *The South Branch of the Potomac*. 1931.

Kemper, C. E. "Documents Relating to Early Projected Swiss Colonies." *Virginia Magazine of History and Biography* 29, no. 1, 1921.

Kercheval, Samuel. *A History of the Valley of Virginia*. Woodstock, Virginia, 1850.

Writers Project, Work Projects Administration. *West Virginia, A Guide to the Mountain State*. New York, 1941.

⟨*estuary*⟩

Facts on the size of the estuary are found in:

Potomac Planning Task Force, U.S. Department of the Interior. *The Potomac*. Washington, 1967.

## *Tidewater Colonial*

The following sources were used in this chapter:

Beitzell, Edwin W. *Life on the Potomac River*. Washington, 1968.

Beverley, Robert. *The History and Present State of Virginia*. Chapel Hill, 1947.

Burnaby, Andrew. *Travels Through North America*. New York, 1904.

Byrd, William. *William Byrd's Natural History of Virginia*. Richmond, 1940.

Durand of Dauphiné. *A Huguenot Exile in Virginia*. New York, 1934.

Fitzpatrick, J. C., ed. *The Diaries of George Washington*. Boston and New York, 1925.

———. *The Writings of George Washington*. Washington, 1931–44.

Freeman, Douglas Southall. *George Washington*. New York, 1948.

Hening, W. W. *Virginia Laws, Statutes, Etc.* New York, 1819–23.
Jefferson, Thomas. *Notes on the State of Virginia.* New York, 1964.
Lear, Tobias. *Observations of the River Potomack.* Baltimore, 1940.
Mereness, N. D., ed. *Travels in the American Colonies.* New York, 1916.
Morrison, A. J., ed. *Travels in Virginia in Revolutionary Times.* Lynchburg, 1922.
Scharf, J. T. *History of Maryland.* Hatboro, Pennsylvania, 1967.
Schoepf, Johann David. *Travels in the Confederation.* Philadelphia, 1911.
Slaughter, Philip. *The History of Truro Parish in Virginia.* Philadelphia, 1908.
Smyth, J. F. D. *Tour in the United States.* London, 1784.
Watkins, C. Malcolm. "The Cultural History of Marlborough, Virginia." Bulletin no. 253. Smithsonian Institution, Washington, 1968.
Williams, John R., ed. *Philip Vickers Fithian, Journal and Letters.* Princeton, 1900.

## Turning Point: 1776

The Revolutionary War on the Potomac was researched from:
Beitzell, Edwin W. *Life on the Potomac River.* Washington, 1968.
Scharf, J. T. *History of Maryland.* Hatboro, Pennsylvania, 1967.

## Upriver Settlement

The first two sections of this chapter are taken from the following sources:
Burnaby, Andrew. *Travels Through North America.* New York, 1904.
Fitzpatrick, J. C., ed. *The Diaries of George Washington.* Boston and New York, 1925.
————. *The Writings of George Washington.* Washington, 1931–44.
Harrison, Fairfax. *Landmarks of Old Prince William.* Richmond, 1924.
McAtee, W. L. *A Sketch of the Natural History of the District of Columbia.* Washington, 1918.
Smyth, J. F. D. *Tour in the United States.* London, 1784.
The journal of the Moravian brothers is found in:
Mereness, N. D., ed. *Travels in the American Colonies.* New York, 1916.

Meshach Browning's experiences are from:

Browning, Meshach. *Forty-four Years the Life of a Hunter*. Philadelphia, 1859.

The following sources provided material for the balance of the chapter:

Amelung, John F. *Remarks on Manufactures, Principally on the New Established Glass-House*. Frederick-Town, 1787.

Binns, John A. *A Treatise on Practical Farming*. Frederick-Town, 1803.

Cunz, Dieter. *The Maryland Germans*. Princeton, 1948.

Harrison, Fairfax. *Landmarks of Old Prince William*. Richmond, 1924.

Jefferson, Thomas. *Notes on the State of Virginia*. New York, 1964.

Kercheval, Samuel. *A History of the Valley of Virginia*. Woodstock, Virginia, 1850.

Morrison, A. J., ed. *Travels in Virginia in Revolutionary Times*. Lynchburg, 1922.

Quynn, Dorothy. "Johann Friedrich Amelung at New Bremen." *Maryland Historical Magazine* 43: 155–179.

## ⟨*geology*⟩

The material on Potomac geology is taken from these sources:

Butts, Charles. "Geology of the Appalachian Valley in Virginia." Bulletin no. 52. Virginia Geological Survey, Charlottesville, 1936.

Butts, C.; Stose, G. W.; and Jonas, A. I. *Southern Appalachian Region*. U.S. Geological Survey, Washington, 1933.

National Park Service, U.S. Department of the Interior. Brochure, "Shenandoah National Park."

Potomac Planning Task Force, U.S. Department of the Interior. *The Potomac*. Washington, 1967.

Scharf, J. T. *History of Maryland*. Hatboro, Pennsylvania, 1967.

Stose, G. W.; Jonas, A. I.; and Ashley, G. H. *Southern Pennsylvania and Maryland*. Washington, 1932.

U.S. Department of Agriculture. *Potomac River Drainage Basin*. Washington, 1943.

Vokes, H. E. "Geography and Geology of Maryland." Bulletin no. 19. Department of Geology, Mines and Water Resources, Baltimore, 1957.

Writers Project, Work Projects Administration. *Virginia, A Guide to the Old Dominion*. New York, 1941.

## Federal City

Material dealing with establishment of the District of Columbia, and with Pierre L'Enfant, is taken from the following:

Bryan, Wilhelmus B. *A History of the National Capital*. New York, 1914.

Caemmerer, H. P. *A Manual on the Origin and Development of Washington*. Washington, 1939.

Fitzpatrick, J. C., ed. *The Diaries of George Washington*. Boston and New York, 1925.

———. *The Writings of George Washington*. Washington, 1931–44.

Kite, Elizabeth S. *L'Enfant and Washington, 1791–1792*. Baltimore, 1929.

*L'Enfant's Reports to President Washington* . . . Columbia Historical Society Records, vol. 2.

Nicolay, Helen. *Our Capital on the Potomac*. New York and London, 1924.

Padover, S. K., ed. *Thomas Jefferson and the National Capital*. Washington, 1946.

Material dealing with the War of 1812 and the burning of the capital is taken from:

Scharf, J. T. *History of Maryland*. Hatboro, Pennsylvania, 1967.

These two sources provide the conclusion of the chapter:

Audubon Society of the District of Columbia. *Washington: City in the Woods*. Washington, 1954.

Bryan, George S. *The Great American Myth*. New York, 1940.

## ⟨interdigitation⟩

This paragraph is derived from:

McAtee, W. L. *A Sketch of the National History of the District of Columbia*. Washington, 1918.

Writers Project, Work Projects Administration. *Maryland, A Guide to the Old Line State*. New York, 1940.

## Transportation

Material on the Ohio Company and Nemacolin's Path is from the following:

Bacon-Foster, Cora. *Early Chapters in the Development of the Potomac Route to the West*. Washington, 1912.

Bailey, Kenneth. *The Ohio Company of Virginia and the Westward Movement, 1748–1792*. Glendale, California, 1939.

Bailey, Kenneth. *Thomas Cresap, Maryland Frontiersman*. Boston, 1944.

Hanna, Charles. *The Wilderness Trail*. New York, 1911.

The section dealing with Braddock is from:

Beitzell, Edwin W. *Life on the Potomac River*. Washington, 1968.

Hulbert, A. B. *Braddock's Road*. Cleveland, 1903.

Two sources provided material for the National Road:

Hulbert, A. B. *The Cumberland Road*. Cleveland, 1904.

Searight, Thomas. *The Old Pike*. Uniontown, Pennsylvania, 1894.

Material on the Potomac Company is derived from the following:

Bacon-Foster, Cora. *Early Chapters in the Development of the Potomac Route to the West*. Washington, 1912.

Davis, Julia. *The Shenandoah*. New York, 1945.

Fitzpatrick, J. C., ed. *The Diaries of George Washington*. Boston and New York, 1925.

———. *The Writings of George Washington*. Washington, 1931–44.

Hulbert, A. B. *The Great American Canals*. Cleveland, 1904.

McCardell, Lee. "Canal Boat Days." *Baltimore Evening Sun,* August 9–13, 1937.

National Park Service and Fairfax County Park Authority. Brochure, "Great Falls of the Potomac."

Sanderlin, Walter S. *The Great National Project: A History of the Chesapeake & Ohio Canal*. Baltimore, 1946.

Description of the Chesapeake and Ohio Canal is drawn from the following sources:

Bacon-Foster, Cora. *Early Chapters in the Development of the Potomac Route to the West*. Washington, 1912.

Hulbert, A. B. *The Great American Canals*. Cleveland, 1904.

McCardell, Lee. "Canal Boat Days." *Baltimore Evening Sun,* August 9–13, 1937.

National Park Service, U.S. Department of the Interior. *Proposed Potomac National River*. Washington, 1968.

"Regulations for Navigating the Chesapeake and Ohio Canal." U.S. Department of the Interior Archives, no date.

Sanderlin, Walter S. *The Great National Project: A History of the Chesapeake & Ohio Canal*. Baltimore, 1946.

⟨*climate and flow—land use*⟩

Material in this section is from the following:

Federal Interdepartmental Task Force on the Potomac, U.S. Department of the Interior. *Land, People and Recreation in the Potomac River Basin*. Washington, 1968.

U.S. Army Corps of Engineers. *Potomac River and Tributaries, Maryland, Virginia, West Virginia*. Washington, 1946.

U.S. Department of Agriculture. *The Potomac River Drainage Basin*. Washington, 1943.

## Civil War

JOHN BROWN

The John Brown story is derived from:

Brown, John. *Words of John Brown*. Boston, 1897.

Bryan, George S. *The Great American Myth*. New York, 1940.

Forbes, John Murray. *Letters and Recollections*. Boston and New York, 1899.

*Frank Leslie's Illustrated Newspaper,* December 10, 1859.

Hart, A. B., ed. *American History Told by Contemporaries*. New York, 1931.

Ruchames, Louis, ed. *A John Brown Reader*. New York, 1959.

Villard, Oswald Garrison. *John Brown, 1800–1859.* Boston and New York, 1910.

Warren, Robert Penn. *John Brown*. New York, 1929.

BULL RUN

Following are the sources for First Bull Run, or First Manassas:

Blackford, W. W. *War Years with Jeb Stuart*. New York, 1945.

Casler, John O. *Four Years in the Stonewall Brigade*. Girard, Kansas, 1906.

Eisenschiml, Otto, and Newman, Ralph, eds. *The American Iliad*. Indianapolis, 1947.

Hanson, J. M. *Bull Run Remembers*. Washington, 1953.

Johnson, R. U., and Buel, C. C., eds. *Battles and Leaders of the Civil War*. New York, 1887–88.

Johnston, David E. *The Story of a Confederate Boy in the Civil War*. Portland, Oregon, 1914.

LaBree, Ben, ed. *The Confederate Soldier in the Civil War*. Louisville, 1895.

*War of the Rebellion: A Compilation of the Official Records of the Union and Confederate Armies*. Washington, 1902.

A SMALL ENGAGEMENT

The affair at Hanging Rocks is described in:

Johnston, C. H. L., ed. *The South Branch of the Potomac*. 1931.

BALL'S BLUFF

Following are the sources for the battle of Ball's Bluff— or Leesburg, as the Confederates called it:

Johnson, R. U., and Buel, C. C., eds. *Battles and Leaders of the Civil War*. New York, 1887–88.

Pierson, Charles L. *Ball's Bluff, An Episode and Its Consequences to Some of Us*. Salem, Massachusetts, 1913.

Quint, Alonzo H. *The Potomac and the Rapidan*. Boston, 1864.

Shotwell, R. A. *Papers of . . .* Raleigh, 1929.

*War of the Rebellion: A Compilation of the Official Records of the Union and Confederate Armies*. Washington, 1902.

SPRINGTIME

Quint, Alonzo H. *The Potomac and the Rapidan*. Boston, 1864.

ANTIETAM

Accounts of Antietam—or Sharpsburg—come from the following:

Alexander, E. P. *Military Memoirs of a Confederate*. New York, 1907.

Blackford, W. W. *War Years with Jeb Stuart*. New York, 1945.

Douglas, Henry Kyd. *I Rode with Stonewall*. Chapel Hill, 1940.

Durkin, Joseph T., ed. *John Dooley, Confederate Soldier: His War Journal*. Washington, 1945.

Eisenschiml, Otto, and Newman, Ralph, eds. *The American Iliad*. Indianapolis, 1947.

Freeman, Douglas Southall. *Lee's Lieutenants*. New York, 1942–44.

Hart, A. B., ed. *American History Told by Contemporaries*. New York, 1931.

Heysinger, Isaac W. *Antietam and the Maryland and Virginia Campaigns of 1862*. New York, 1912.

Hood, J. B. *Advance and Retreat*. New Orleans, 1880.

Johnson, R. U., and Buel, C. C., eds. *Battles and Leaders of the Civil War*. New York, 1887–88.

Johnston, David E. *The Story of a Confederate Boy in the Civil War*. Portland, Oregon, 1914.

LaBree, Ben, ed. *The Confederate Soldier in the Civil War*. Louisville, 1895.

Napier, Bartlett. *A Soldier's Story of the War*. New Orleans, 1874.

Noyes, George F. *The Bivouac and the Battlefield*. New York, 1863.

Owen, W. M. *In Camp and Battle with the Washington Artillery of New Orleans*. New Orleans, 1964.

Page, C. D. *History of the 14th Regiment, Connecticut Volunteer Infantry*. Meriden, Connecticut, 1906.

Quint, Alonzo H. *The Potomac and the Rapidan*. Boston, 1864.

Shotwell, R. A. *Papers of*. . . Raleigh, 1929.

Writers Project, Work Projects Administration. *Maryland, A Guide to the Old Line State*. New York, 1940.

GETTYSBURG

The Battle of Gettysburg is derived from the following:

Aldrich, T. M. *History of Battery A, First Regiment, Rhode Island Light Artillery*. Providence, 1904.

Alexander, E. P. *Military Memoirs of a Confederate*. New York, 1907.

Blackford, W. W. *War Years with Jeb Stuart*. New York, 1945.

Casler, John O. *Four Years in the Stonewall Brigade*. Girard, Kansas, 1906.

Durkin, Joseph T., ed. *John Dooley, Confederate Soldier: His War Journal*. Washington, 1945.

Eisenschiml, Otto, and Newman, Ralph, eds. *The American Iliad*. Indianapolis, 1947.

Fremantle, Arthur L. *The Fremantle Diary*. Boston, 1954.

Harrison, Walter. *Pickett's Men*. New York, 1870.

Hart, A. B., ed. *American History Told by Contemporaries*. New York, 1931.

Haskell, Frank, A. *The Battle of Gettysburg*. Boston, 1958.

Johnson, R. U., and Buel, C. C., eds. *Battles and Leaders of the Civil War*. New York, 1887–88.

Johnston, David E. *The Story of a Confederate Boy in the Civil War*. Portland, Oregon, 1914.

Kimble, June. "Tennesseans at Gettysburg: The Retreat." *Confederate Veteran*, October, 1910.

King, John R. *My Experience in the Confederate Army and in Northern Prisons*. Clarksburg, West Virginia, 1917.

LaBree, Ben, ed. *The Confederate Soldier in the Civil War*. Louisville, 1895.

McClure, A. K., ed. *The Annals of the War*. Philadelphia, 1879.

Miers, E. S., and Brown, R. A., eds. *Gettysburg*. New Brunswick, 1948.

Napier, Bartlett. *A Soldier's Story of the War*. New Orleans, 1874.

Page, C. D. *History of the 14th Regiment, Connecticut Volunteer Infantry*. Meriden, Connecticut, 1906.

Pickett, LaSalle Corbell. *Pickett and His Men*. Atlanta, 1899.

Rhodes, John H. *The Gettysburg Gun*. No. 19. Rhode Island Soldiers & Sailors Historical Society.

Shotwell, R. A. *Papers of . . .* Raleigh, 1929.

Stewart, George. *Pickett's Charge*. Boston, 1959.

PRISONERS OF WAR

The account of Point Lookout is from the following:

Keiley, Anthony M. *In Vinculis*. New York, 1866.

King, John R. *My Experience in the Confederate Army and in Northern Prisons*. Clarksburg, West Virginia, 1917.

Pierson, W. W., ed. *Diary of Bartlett Yancey Malone*. Chapel Hill, 1919.

Shotwell, R. A. *Papers of . . .* Raleigh, 1929.

*War of the Rebellion: A Compilation of the Official Records of the Union and Confederate Armies*. Washington, 1902.

APRIL 1865

The Lincoln assassination story is derived from the following:

Bryan, George S. *The Great American Myth*. New York, 1940.

DeWitt, David M. *The Assassination of Abraham Lincoln*. New York, 1909.

Jones, Thomas A. *J. Wilkes Booth*. Chicago, 1893.

Stern, Philip Van Doren. *The Man Who Killed Lincoln*. New York, 1939.

## Nineteen Sixties

ONE

The items dealing with Rafinesque (or Schmaltz) are taken from:

Call, R. E. *Life and Writings of Rafinesque*. Louisville, 1895.

Interstate Commission on the Potomac River Basin. *Potomac Playlands*. Washington, 1957.

Rafinesque, C. S. *A Life of Travels and Researches . . .* Philadelphia, 1836.

TWO

The geology and geography of the area were researched from among the following:

Bevan, Arthur. "Origin of Our Scenery." Bulletin no. 46–A. Virginia Geological Survey.

Butts, Charles. "Geology of the Appalachian Valley in Virginia." Bulletin no. 52. Virginia Geological Survey.

Butts, C.; Stose, G. W.; and Jonas, A. I. *Southern Appalachian Region.* U.S. Geological Survey, Washington, 1933.

Davis, Julia. *The Shenandoah.* New York, 1945.

McAtee, W. L. *A Sketch of the Natural History of the District of Columbia.* Washington, 1918.

National Park Service, U.S. Department of the Interior, brochure, "Shenandoah National Park."

Smith, J. Lawrence. *The Potomac Naturalist.* Parsons, West Virginia, 1968.

Vokes, H. E. *Geography and Geology of Maryland.* Bulletin no. 19. Department of Geology, Mines and Water Resources, Baltimore, 1957.

Writers Project, Work Projects Administration. *Virginia, A Guide to the Old Dominion.* New York, 1941.

The material dealing with Potomac flora and fauna is derived from the following:

Gilbert, Bil. "Exaltations at the Smokehole." *Sports Illustrated,* April 27, 1964.

Halle, Louis J. *Spring in Washington.* New York, 1963.

McAtee and Weed. "First List of the Fishes in the Vicinity of Plummer's Island, Maryland." *Proceedings of the Biological Society of Washington,* vol. 28, 1915.

Potomac-side Naturalists' Club. *Flora Columbiana.* Washington, 1876.

Sharpe, G., and Sharpe, W. *101 Wildflowers of Shenandoah National Park.* Seattle, 1958.

Shosteck, Robert. *The Potomac Trail Book.* Washington, 1935.

Smith, J. Lawrence. *The Potomac Naturalist.* Parsons, West Virginia, 1968.

Taylor, John W. "The Wicomico River." *Atlantic Naturalist* 9, no. 3, January–February, 1954.

THREE

Following are sources on Potomac pollution:

Beitzell, Edwin W. *Life on the Potomac River.* Washington, 1968.

Bradley, M. *An Ecological Survey of the Potomac and Anacostia Rivers.* Washington, 1959.

Bureau of Business and Economic Research, University of Maryland. *Potomac River Basin.* College Park, 1957.

Coordinating Committee on the Potomac River Valley. *Potomac Prospect.* Washington, 1961.

Durum, W. H., and Langbein, W. B. *Water Quality of the Potomac River Estuary at Washington, D.C.* Circular no. 529–A. U.S. Geological Survey, Washington, 1966.

Environmental Pollution Panel, President's Science Advisory Committee. *Restoring the Quality of Our Environment.* Washington, 1965.

Federal Water Pollution Control Administration, U.S. Department of the Interior. *Wastewater Inventory, Upper Potomac River Basin.* Washington, 1969.

Interstate Commission on the Potomac River Basin. *Report on Industrial Wastes in the Potomac River Basin.* Washington, 1950.

———. *Soils Pollution in the Potomac River Basin.* Washington, 1949.

Lear, Tobias. *Observations on the River Potomack.* Baltimore, 1940.

*New York Times* News Service.

Potomac Planning Task Force, U.S. Department of the Interior. *The Potomac.* Washington, 1967.

Smyth, J. F. D. *Tour in the United States.* London, 1784.

U.S. Department of the Interior. *Potomac Interim Report to the President.* Washington, 1966.

U.S. Department of the Interior. *The Nation's River.* Washington, 1968.

FOUR

Facts on military land use are taken from:

Project Potomac, U.S. Department of the Interior. *Potomac Valley.* Washington, 1966.

FIVE

President Johnson's message, and the plans of the Corps of Engineers, are taken from:

Federal Water Pollution Control Administration, U.S. Department of the Interior. *Mine Drainage in the North Branch Potomac River Basin.* Washington, 1969.

Kindleberger, B. "Should the Potomac Be Dammed?" *American Forests,* August, 1957.

U.S. Government Printing Office. "Beauty for America." *Proceedings of the White House Conference on Natural Beauty*. Washington.

SEVEN

Sources for this section are the following:

Calhoun, J. B. "The Social Aspects of Population Dynamics." *Journal of Mammalogy* 33 (1952).

Fitzpatrick, J. C., ed. *The Writings of George Washington*. Washington, 1931–44.

Hall, Edward T. *The Hidden Dimension*. Garden City, 1966.

U.S. Department of the Interior. *Potomac Interim Report to the President*. Washington, 1966.

*Washington Post*, April 6, 1968.

EIGHT

Following are sources for this final section:

Durham, C. J. S. *Washington's Potowmack Canal Project at Great Falls*. The Nature Conservancy, Washington, 1957.

Fairfax County Park Authority and National Park Service. Brochure, "Great Falls of the Potomac."

Fosberg, Raymond. Private conversation.

Interstate Commission on the Potomac River Basin. *Potomac Playlands*. Washington, 1957.

McAtee, W. L. *A Sketch of the Natural History of the District of Columbia*. Washington, 1918.

Design by David Bullen
Typeset in Mergenthaler Bembo
by Wilsted & Taylor
Printed by Maple-Vail
on acid-free paper